Max J. Friedländer

Reminiscences
and Reflections

Friedländer as assistant of the Kaiser Friedrich Museum, between
Wilhelm von Bode (right) and Hauser, the restorer, 1904

Max J. Friedländer

Reminiscences and Reflections

*Edited from the literary remains and with
a foreword by* Rudolf M. Heilbrunn

New York Graphic Society Ltd.

Greenwich, Connecticut

Translated from the German

by Ruth S. Magurn

© 1969 New York Graphic Society Ltd.

SBN 8212-1109-9

Library of Congress Catalog Card No. 68-25741

Printed and bound in the United States of America by

The Book Press, Division of General Educational Services Corp.

Design by Peter Oldenburg

Contents

List of Illustrations

Foreword

IF ONE VISITED Geheimrat Max J. Friedländer during
the late years of the war and the first years thereafter in his apart-
ment in Amsterdam, one might well come upon him writing. With
his neat, scholarly script he covered octavo sheets, which he concealed in a pasteboard box. What the content of these notes was
remained hidden from the visitor. Nevertheless, the conversation,
which covered the most diverse subjects, might well be a continuation of these notes. The events of the day were, in these years of
world change, almost never spoken of (very much in contrast to talks
with Max Beckmann, who lived not far from Friedländer), but
often the subjects considered were connected with what he had been
reading. Once, for example, in alluding to Carl Justi's great
biography, Friedländer remarked how fortunate Winckelmann was
to have found two writers like Goethe and Justi as biographers; or,
again and again, the Geheimrat referred to Schopenhauer, whose
style he praised more than his philosophical views. I have later
often regretted that I did not write down the remarks of Friedländer while they were fresh in my memory. But among his literary
remains were found those scraps of paper which seem to me today
like a distillation of these conversations. In them Friedländer has
to some extent summed up a ninety-year life, and thus they may be
regarded as the legacy of the connoisseur and the researcher.

Besides the true aphorisms, there were found the brief reminiscences of Friedländer's youth, as well as those on Wilhelm von
Bode and the Berlin collectors of the late nineteenth century. In
these notes one will see, beyond the personal, a contribution to the
picture of that city in whose artistic life the longtime director of

9

the Berlin Print Room played so important a role as Bode's helper. For when Friedländer in the foreword to his principal work, the *Altniederländische Malerei,* states that he grew up in Berlin in a house hardly two hundred meters distant from the Altes Museum, one will be able to perceive in that proximity a doubly symbolic meaning; he was, in fact, the "genuine Berliner," intimately familiar from early youth with the artistic tendencies of the city of Schadow and Rauch, of Menzel and Liebermann. He was descended from an old Berlin family of jewellers, just as so many of the Netherlandish and Early German masters investigated by him stemmed from goldsmiths, and the connoisseurship which Friedländer modestly believed must be attributed to association with experienced museum men and collectors may have rested, not least, upon the "hereditary faculty" which fathers and forefathers had acquired in the collecting and mounting of precious stones, in the forming and fashioning of costly vessels and ornamental pieces. Perhaps the reader of the aphorisms will be reminded of the jeweller's handiwork in many of the polished *aperçus.* These talents and attributes inherited from his fathers were supplemented by a maternal inheritance which brought an admixture of South German color to the Berlin sobriety. For Friedländer was descended on his mother's side from that Goldschmidt family of Frankfurt which can point to so many members prominent in German culture and science. The words of Goethe apply in a high degree also to Friedländer: "When families maintain themselves for a long time, one can observe that nature finally brings forth an individual whose personality comprehends the characteristic qualities of his collective ancestors, uniting and completely expressing all the hitherto isolated and indicated tendencies." In Friedländer and in his scientific and administrative work there were concentrated, as in a burning-glass, efforts and achievements by which those two Berlin and Frankfurt families, and others, expressed their debt to German culture

10

and demonstrated their native right in the realm of Goethe and Jacob Burckhardt. What is clear to those who know the writings of Friedländer becomes discernible anew from our notes: namely, that Friedländer's theoretical and scientific production grew out of the experience and connoisseurship of the practitioner, like that of the fathers of German writing on art, Sandrart, Winckelmann, Fiorello, Rumohr, Waagen, Bode, Lichtwark. But at the same time there is demonstrated how very much "the breadth of his interests was limited by a principle that is best expressed by the English word 'selectivity,' " as Erwin Panofsky has formulated it.

Bode, in the foreword to a bibliography of Friedländer's scholarly works that appeared in 1927 (on the occasion of Friedländer's sixtieth birthday), evaluated with warm words the activity of Friedländer "in the building up, the arrangement, and the scientific elaboration" of the Berlin Gallery. Yet even for the museum director posterity wreathes no garlands. The work of the creators and shapers of the Berlin Museum-Island is today shattered and dis-membered, as is the city of Berlin. How very closely Friedländer was bound to the Berlin Museums, even after the painful experiences of his emigration to the hospitable land of Descartes and Spinoza, became clear to me on the occasion of the Amsterdam exhibition in 1950 of the paintings of the former Kaiser Friedrich Museum, when I saw the impression the works of art made on their onetime curator and augmenter. When these "fugitives from the East," on their Ahasueran wandering through the Old and New Worlds, reached the city of Rembrandt, it seemed not so much the joy of seeing again old friends and loved ones that affected Friedländer, as the consciousness of seeing these beloved objects that he had once guarded and cared for snatched from their ancestral and accustomed home and expatriated—seeing them naked and bare, without the frames Bode had assembled with love, care, and connoisseurship, far from the milieu the great collector and organizer had created on the Museum-Island with so much taste and understanding. For the Geheimrat it was perhaps like seeing again, in late years, one dearly and constantly loved since early youth, whom fate and the present had torn away and hurled out of the orbit of her star.

Shattered and dismembered are the work and achievement of Bode, Lippmann, and Friedländer in their museum activity. Unforgotten, however, across the years there will stand as a monument more enduring than bronze the one that Friedländer has erected with the corpus of the *Altniederländische Malerei*. For as the names 'Bartsch,' 'Nagler,' 'Schreiber,' have become concepts for amateurs of early graphic art, as 'Brunet,' 'Graesse,' 'Lowndes' for booklovers, so has 'the Friedländer' become an indispensable possession for everyone occupied with early North European panel painting. In this magnum opus Friedländer has presented to contemporaries as on a silver platter, and has handed down to posterity, the ripe fruits of a century of scientific art collecting and research. It may only be noted—in order to designate the merit of this work—that perhaps for the beginnings of Italian panel painting a corresponding work is lacking, in spite of the significant investigations of Berenson, Venturi, and Van Marle.

Yet when Friedländer, in the foreword to the masterwork of 1923, modestly remarked that he had for about thirty-five years been "uninterruptedly concerned with one and the same thing," namely, looking at Netherlandish painting, one will be able to concur with this 'expertise' only with reservation. "Here Friedländer is mistaken." For even a hastly leafing through the bibliographies of 1927, 1942, and 1957 shows a truly polyphonic roster of themes. As early as the year 1888 there is a work entitled *Zola and Plein-Air Painting,* a subject whose treatment one would perhaps not have expected from the connoisseur and researcher of the Netherlandish Primitives. The aphorisms also demonstrate that Friedländer's sphere of interests did not embrace only early Netherlandish

12

painting. One realizes rather, from these notes, how much Friedländer's thoughts included themes which appear to be far removed from true art scholarship. Above all it becomes clear that the development of language was a particular concern of the writer who also in his essay, "On Foreign Words" (in the *Deutsche Rundschau* of August, 1919), had called to mind that the German spirit was to be understood in the mirror of the language.

And so these paralipomena may be taken not only as a supplement to the learned works of the great connoisseur and researcher, but also as the testament of a generation whose work and whose achievement, in the shadow of tomorrow, often seem to be thrown into the shade today.

RUDOLF M. HEILBRUNN

Max J. Friedländer

Reminiscences
and Reflections

Ego

WITH A PESSIMISTIC imagination, I have anticipated difficulties and painted them very black to myself. For that reason I have never, even in comfortable circumstances, felt really happy. My capacity for enjoyment was little developed, whereas reverses, when they occurred, I was able to bear relatively easily, often with the feeling: "Nothing further," or "I imagined it worse." In old age, after the loss of fortune, of family, the possibility of effective work, social position, I feel no more oppressed than I did in youth and middle age, than in the period when, as it seemed to others, I lived in the most fortunate circumstances.

This disposition accounts for the fact that I have avoided responsibilities, but as soon as I felt myself obliged to discharge a task, I have done it accurately, carefully, and conscientiously. I have made more mistakes of omission than of commission.

(On the other hand: He who cannot say "no" becomes the slave of Everyman. Something like this in Montaigne.)

As a Jew, I considered myself at a disadvantage in my youth, with limited prospects, and I adapted myself to this situation. Later the current of time bore me upward, since between 1895 and 1914, and then between 1918 and 1925, the Jews in Germany, and particularly in Berlin, made remarkable advances in many fields, such as the press, the theater, and administration. This was not so much because of increased strength as in consequence of diminished opposition. The fateful effect of this expansion of power, the harsh backlash, was manifest after 1930. It was those successes that made the Führer's anti-Semitism so seductive.

17

When, with an objectivity that is given me—a wise man once said that I was morbidly objective—I look upon my lack of classical education and lack of diligence, on the one hand, and on the other upon my successes, the authority I have attained, the respect I have won without striving for it, I must come to the conclusion that I was endowed with a specific, one-sided gift, and I must highly appreciate certain powers, such as visual memory, a bent for connoisseurship, as well as capacity as a writer. Within myself I was conscious of these advantages, so that with all modesty in attitude, I did not lack intellectual pride, a feeling of superiority. Tolerant, confident in the society of unimportant contemporaries, reserved and uncommunicative toward stronger personalities, without talent for friendship, I have lived in spiritual isolation.

Reminiscences about Bode

I KNEW Wilhelm Bode well, since I was close to him for decades and was for a long time active under him as assistant. In any case I knew him better than he knew me. This is because the servant, the subordinate, knows more about his master than the master about the servant. Moreover Bode, with sis eminently active nature, was not a good observer and no judge of men. He thought well of me. Otherwise he would not have appointed me as his successor. I believe, however, that it was rather my weaknesses than my strong points that commended me to him. In his eyes—and not in his only—I lacked initiative and a will of my own. Bode may have felt and expected that I would carry on his work conservatively and thoroughly according to his views. He was suspicious of independent impulses in his staff of co-workers. His antipathy, his very hostile attitude toward colleagues, directors of other museums, who did not subordinate themselves to him, who did not obey his instructions, asserted itself with some regularity. Thus he fell out with Von Tschudi, and opposed Pauli, Swarzenski and others with sharp judgment.

Quick at repartee in conversation, not infrequently overbearingly aggressive, he was embarrassed and unable to reprimand his subordinates, whiel toward those absent he often expressed himself immoderately. Toward his superiors he was nervously tense, if not hostile, and he made life harder for them than for his subordinates. This is a feature of an aristocratic mind.

Bode's image hovers before me as that of a medium-sized, lean, sinewy man, agile and with a talent for sport. He was an ardent mountain climber, although no longer at the time when I came to know him. From 1896 he was periodically ill, never quite healthy, but his enormous energy for work was nevertheless impaired to a remarkably small degree. The constant anxiety for his health became for him an expedient in avoiding many a diversion or obligation, and in devoting himself with a more single-minded purpose to his narrowly defined mission in life.

Coming from the Harz region, descendant of an upper middle class family which had produced able and aspiring public officials, he held to strict, Protestant, puritanical principles which, however, did not direct his actions, but merely defined his judgment on the actions of others. In his own actions he was completely free from principles, even guilelessly without conscience in his dealings.

He was decidedly Germanic in racial type, blond, with a knife-sharp nose, soldierly, although not robust. He appeared threatening, and was able all the more, when he wished, to win over visitors to himself and his ends by unexpected friendliness and confidence.

Many a person entered his office with trepidation, but left it in high spirits, under the impression that he, and only he as an exception, enjoyed the confidence of such an exalted and demanding personality.

As to Bode's mentality: He possessed a relatively large portfolio of stock certificates, and asked an experienced merchant for advice, whether he should hold on to the paper or sell it. The advice was: "Sell half of it." Bode found this advice absurd and ridiculed it. He knew only of good values and bad, and presumed that an expert must know which was good and which was bad. Careful calculation in order to reduce risk was to him incomprehensible.

Bode had at his disposal a thoroughly reliable visual memory, an ambition amounting to genius, directed solely toward the enrichment of the State Collections. And for half a century instrumental for the Berlin Museums, at times favored by political and economic conditions, he accomplished more than any other museum director for any other institution. His extensive literary activity, which was

20

Wilhelm von Bode, *Portrait by Max Liebermann, 1909*

strictly connected with the practical activity of acquisition and the building up of the collections, has in itself relatively slight importance and is hardly of lasting value. Unhesitatingly ready with an answer, in writing as well as orally, Bode gave an opinion on art works from many fields, on Netherlandish painting of the seventeenth century, on Italian sculpture, Persian rugs, majolica, German wood sculpture, and many other things. His writings were for him always a means to an end, and were frequently controversial and advocatory. Almost always he judged correctly, and at the time he expressed them, his communications were of significance and infinitely enriched knowledge in many fields. But the tragic fate of the "connoisseur" lies in the fact that yesterday's new, strikingly accurate definitions are today's common property and banalities, that only the mistakes linger in the memory under the name of the originator. Leonardo's wax bust, which seems to many a blunder of Bode's, is still occasionally mentioned, while the overwhelming majority of the unerring judgments which turned out successfully for the connoisseur ever ready to plunge have become a matter of course, anonymous, no longer bringing credit to the originator.

Bode was not a writer in the true sense, not so much because he lacked the capacity for it—he occasionally expressed himself vividly, especially in letters—as because he never considered what constituted the task of the writer on art. Completely uncritical in literary matters, he hardly ever changed a word, crossed out a sentence. His capacity to grasp nuances of feeling in words was little developed. That it might be his task to cultivate this capacity never occurred to him. The more refined the artistic judgment— and his was, as facts proved, refined to a high degree—the more pressing the need to bring the verbal expression in some measure to the same level. One cannot with twenty words do justice to the infinite richness of the artistic impression. In reading an essay of Bode's one learns from it that he considers a certain picture the work of Rembrandt. This was once important, but is so no longer, because everyone now knows it. But the sentences by which he might have convinced the reader of the accuracy of his judgment contain next to nothing of that which determined the judgment. They sound trivial, as though written by someone who had a great deal less experience in front of Rembrandt's works than Bode had.

Although Bode was extremely learned in many branches of art history and had his information always ready—he had little need of written notes and photographs—he was no scholar in the true sense. He was more fond of action than of reflection, and was far from having a just and objective mind. Moreover, the distracting practice of uninterrupted daily work hindered a comprehensive synthesis of realization. The deepest motive of the scholar, namely, disinterested love of truth, could not function productively in a nature always resolutely aiming for effectiveness and visible results. Bode was utterly unphilosophical, he considered no affair from more than one side. He saw black or white, good or bad, advantageous or inimical; he knew no intermediary steps. To foresee obstacles, to fear, to guard against them, was not his way. Consequently he became angry as soon as he encountered opposition. He made more mistakes by acting than by failing to act. He was a hunter, not an angler.

The picture of Bode would be incomplete if I did not speak of the mirror in which he thus appears. And I am that mirror. I go on, therefore, to the frankly ticklish and questionable task of speaking about myself.

Bode was a generation older than I. Nevertheless, I sometimes had the feeling of being older than he was; in any case, I more than he possessed something of indifference, skepticism, resignation, the qualities that mount with the years but which were still not to be noted in him when he was eighty. In these and other respects we were poles apart; I was so alien to him that intimacy did not exist between us. Nevertheless, he was kind to me, and a liberal superior, and I was a conscientious and attentive helper to him.

The racial difference and the difference in social background are not to be forgotten. He belonged to a higher class, coming from a family in which entrance into the higher official career was a prerogative, a natural course. I, on the other hand, as a Jew, coming from a family which had known civic emancipation for at most two generations, was still set apart socially. When I chose my profession I did not think of the possibility of ever being able to become a museum official or a university teacher. I recall that when my father questioned me about the object, the goal and purpose, of my studies, I answered: "I want to be a private scholar." Here already was an anxious and pessimistic view into the future—a view that I have never become quite free from. I was not a little surprised, then, at my "career." I have never striven for a post. What I have attained has been granted me without my doing anything. I was never even in a position to strive for something, because I always, though not from real modesty, estimated my worth as slight in the eyes of others. Deep within me I did not estimate my worth as by any means low. After all, who does?

From War-Time and After

IF GOETHE had not published his collected works under his own name, I should like to know how many of them would be attributed to him by historians of literature. Fame raises claims. The best is applied as a yardstick.

Even Goethe would have received a "doppelgänger." Workshop participation, perhaps by Eckermann, would have been demonstrated.

Tolstoy and Schopenhauer, different as they are from one another, have one thing in common: their judgment on Napoleon.

Schopenhauer, at the news of Napoleon's death, is said to have uttered nothing but: "He was too wicked."

Tolstoy's *Power of Darkness* is said to have sold some 250,000 copies in three days. Nothing can so clearly demonstrate the importance of book printing to the outlook on the world, and indirectly to politics.

The invention of printing, the introduction of the potato, were more momentous for the history of mankind than the victories of Napoleon.

Change in the meaning of words in the plural:
Wort—Wörter, Worte (French *mot—parola*)
Ort—Örter, Orte
Mann—Männer, Mannen
Gesicht—Gesichter, Gesichte
Band—Bänder, Bande
Land—Länder, Lande

[SINGULAR]	[PLURAL]
Wort: Word	*Wörter:* Words (unconnected)
	Worte: Words, sayings, terms
Ort: Place, locality	*Örter:* Places, localities
	Orte: Places (figurative), situations
Mann: Man, husband	*Männer:* Men, husbands
	Mannen: Vassals, retainers
Gesicht: Sight, view, face	*Gesichter:* Faces
	Gesichte: Sights, visions, apparitions
Band: Band, ribbon, bond	*Bänder:* Bands, ribbons
	Bande: Bonds, fetters, ties
Land: Land (vs. water), country (vs. city)	*Länder:* Grounds, plots
	Lande: Countries, regions

Peculiarity of the German language?

The objective meaning in contrast to the poetically, sensitively symbolic is differentiated only in the plural.

Wrong: to form the degrees of comparison of all adjectives.
"Full," "perfect" should not be given degrees of comparison.
Neither should many others.

Drawing is related to painting as wit to humor, as intellect to soul.

Cornelius (letter from Schwind). For him there was no genre about which he wished to know nothing at all.

Schinkel (report on the Boisserée Collection):[1] "Canova, coming from the sculptures of the Parthenon, expressed the following opinion under the effect of the art of Van Eyck: 'Every step taken further from the art of Raphael is a step down; on the

26

Max J. Friedländer, *Drawing by Max Liebermann*
Collection of Marianne Feilchenfeldt, Zurich

foundation of Van Eyck, however, there is an infinite structure to be erected.' " So speaks a classicist.

He is too intelligent to have opinions, at least to hold on to opinions, to trust them.

Vexation makes one talkative. Schopenhauer, who otherwise writes precisely and tightly, becomes wordy and repeats himself as soon as he begins to speak of Hegel, Fichte, and Schelling, and uses every occasion to express himself about them at length, vehemently and blusteringly.

Nietzsche as enlightener. In Basel he strikes at Erasmus, at French literature (Montaigne), he vanquishes Schopenhauer, Romanticism, German philology, finally metaphysics and the remainder of Christianity which Schopenhauer has conserved. Basel is German, but beyond the borders of the Reich.

Have read Brandes' book, *Caesar,* and Voltaire's *Apologies.* Heroes set against the dark background of their times. Of the Voltaire book I have obtained only the second volume. Voltaire gives expression to the thoughts which brought forth the Revolution, to the very feelings which produced it. Rousseau. Toward the end of the eighteenth century German conditions seem healthier than the French: favorable after-effect of the Reformation. England still more healthy, as in the administration of law.

"Arbitrary" is a happy combination of will and choice. The opposite: "necessary." That which is made versus that which has grown.

In the language is the spiritual inheritance of the fathers. However, the validity of this heritage lies in the fact that one must earn it in order to possess it.

28

Beauty aids. Those who need them do not use them; those who use them do not need to use them.

The image-maker is a human being, has a human, therefore symmetrically formed body. For centuries the human body, the human face, were the subjects of art forms; symmetry, balance of the parts, remained dominant in the imagination as the condition for visual satisfaction. Associated with pure symmetry, however, was monotony, and to counteract this, the desire arose to provide variety by means of turning the body. This tendency was served by the contrapposoto of the limbs. The later shift to nature in the form of landscape sprang from an eagerness to break free from symmetry.

A landscape picture has a beginning and an end—according to the will of the painter—but a whole it is *not*.

When the painter finds nature "beautiful," this already contains the reason that what he perceives appears to him inimitable, since he strives in vain to realize the vision. He admires what he has not the power to render, he stands before a richness he cannot exhaust.

He finds nature beautiful, who has learned from the artists how to see.

Old man: platonic Casanova.

He who brings with him a feeling for art can without risk listen to academic lectures on art.

The Classic, inherited by the Italians, learned by the French: by Poussin, by the Saxon, Raffael Mengs. The distinction is noticeable. Picasso: music become frozen.

The German victories of 1864, 1866, and 1870 were less the result of military superiority than of shrewd policy (Bismarck). Bad policy makes on the nation military demands it cannot meet. Not guns but brains decide.

Have been reading the memoirs of the German Crown Prince, and have found them instructive in view of the present situation. To be sure, everything has become much worse.

"Belief" is a dubious concept, because belief has the corollary of unbelief. When I say that I believe the moon is inhabited, I let it be known that this is not a certainty, that I do not know, that I cannot know. "I believe" means "I have reason to suppose, I am inclined to imagine, I accept the opinion, the theory." The Christian doctrine of immortality, Hell, and Paradise has, in fact, come to be "believed" only in the above sense. Were it impressed upon the conviction as knowledge, the devout person would willingly have to exchange the doubtful state of earthly existence for that of Paradise, therefore take his own life. But the only one who takes his own life is the person who is determined to exchange a state unbearable to him for a state of nothingness. No one lives as he would live imbued with the truth of the Christian doctrine. The martyrs and hermits do not prove the contrary. Apart from the fact that the saints are purposely invented by the clergy as model ideals, the hermits pray and chastise themselves because they feel morally obliged to combat doubt. They struggle for certainty because they lack certainty.

Hence the question also to be answered, whether H. Bosch "believed" in Hell.

In Shakespeare's dramas there is little of Christianity to be noted. The action is nowhere motivated by faith. The British appear to have been baptized without success.

Christ would have had to die serenely, had He been certain of exchanging the adverse life on earth for existence in Heaven.

How un-Christian is Hamlet's soliloquy, "To be or not to be."

Character is considered a kernel, a constant set of attributes. A better conception is that of possibilities, not necessities. Possibilities of expansion and reaction. Not: the man is courageous, but: he is so constituted that in this situation he appears courageous. Situation, occasion, circumstances work upon and bring this or that characteristic to light. As a human being every man possesses all the human attributes; it is only according to the circumstances that this or that one predominates and becomes evident as determining an action. Constant characters are found only in fiction, not in life. It is impossible to describe the character of a person one knows; it is more possible to invent a character. In describing a character trait I choose words, therefore concepts, and am already descending from the individual to the typical. The number of concepts is relatively small, the number of individuals infinitely large. When I call a man good-natured, I bring him into a category to which millions of men belong. And when, tightening the net, I give his good disposition a special nuance, he still remains part of a class, even though a smaller one. Every character portrayal is a type-casting. The word remains bound to a concept, the concept to the word. The unattainable ideal would be a life history which contained all the influencing factors. Thereby the character would resolve itself. Character definition is possible only with limited knowledge. Acquaintances one fondly imagines he knows, friends already less, his spouse least of all. Tolstoy's wife, after long marriage, said: "I do not know what sort of man he was."

Only with few strokes, like a flash, can one delineate a character.

In novels the secondary figures are stamped more sharply than the hero. One should see character not as static, but as dynamic.

"His memory is as bad as that of a mirror." Witty metaphor, taken from an American magazine.

"No one has made an invention in a field for which he had been systematically trained." A bold statement, but with some truth in it. Assertion of an American inventor.

The painter sees what he wants to paint and can paint; he does not paint that which intrudes upon his field of vision.

Goethe's verse:
> *Über allen Gipfeln*
> *Ist Ruh, . . .*
> *Warte nur, balde*
> *Ruhest du auch.*

Like an inscription under a painting of Ruisdael's.

When our vices or defects have grown so that we can no longer conceal them, we begin to boast about them.
It is the same with old age. Ultimately one begins to boast even about that. Bredius writes under a letter "aet. 83."

Someone can stand so high above the crowd, or think he stands so high, that he cannot, from such a great distance, perceive the distinction between intelligent and stupid, bad and good, in the single figures. He becomes a neutral, tolerant, ironical observer of individuals. He loses the capacity to love and to hate.

One has little prospect of saying something new, and at the same time accurate—"that former ages have not already thought of." Therefore every effort must be made to say clearly, intelligibly, what one may have to say, without the ambition of saying something new.

Have been reading short stories of young Russians who wrote after the Revolution. In part positively communistic, in part satirical, critical in the face of the changed social order.

Have been reading short stories by the American, Wolfe. Remarkably cruel and bloody tales. Intellectual America is apparently on the verge of coming to an understanding with Russia, in the struggle with the surfeited material prosperity of the ruling class. The intensity and perceptiveness of the observation is astonishing— in a morbid disposition?

Art connoisseurship is really not a science, because it provides a man with a living, which proper sciences do not.

He behaves like a gentleman, but not without having considered how a gentleman in his situation would behave; he *is* therefore no gentleman.

Stendhal: "It is dangerous to buy engravings of paintings one sees on one's travels. Soon the engraving forms the sole recollection and destroys the real memory. So has it happened to me with the Sistine Madonna in Dresden. The beautiful engraving by Müller has destroyed it for me, while the bad pastels of Raffael Mengs in the same gallery, of which I have nowhere seen engravings, I still see clearly before me." This ought to be taken note of by the art historians, whose imaginations are filled with photographs, if not halftones.

In Dutch there are two words for color: *verf* and *kleur*. Color

33

as material and color as an effect. Van Gogh in his letters speaks constantly of the colors on his palette, that is, of *verf*. This tendency is to be noticed in his pictures (after a visit to the Van Gogh exhibition in Amsterdam in 1945). He admits frankly that in painting he starts from the given color materials, not from the given colored appearance of nature.

By the way, I find his drawings more convincing than his paintings.

The lion in the wilderness, the lion behind bars, the stuffed lion, the lion of the imagination—the impression each time is different. The aesthetician does well to ponder over these distinctions. The beauty of the wild beast is not visible as long as danger threatens one; it is tempered, diminished, in captivity, extinguished in the stuffed lion, but free and potent in the imagination.

Wise thoughts of famous authors become quoted. For the most part it may be pointed out that the thought is older, that the quoted author has simply formulated it tersely, has made it understandable to us, and give it felicitous expression.

Many art experts who respond sympathetically to talent shy at genius.

Talent is to genius as the moon is to the sun.

Poets write something, authors write about something.

Schiller's characters, in every situation, are as reflective, as rational, intelligent, and spirited as the author in the writing. All his creatures stand intellectually on the same level. They are masks through which his voice is heard.

34

There has been only one art connoisseur who never made himself ridiculous, and he was dumb and could not write.

Schopenhauer's definition of the concept *symbol* is hardly suitable. The distinction between allegory and symbol, which to me seems critical, is not noted. Symbol: something emblematic, that is, speaking directly to the feelings by way of the senses, something abstract mediating between the senses and the feelings. Allegory: an idea mediated by means of imagery.

Wallenstein's monologue in Schiller's drama: as though a learned historian had made the hero's position clear to himself, composed an admirable treatise on it, and put it into ingenious verse. How differently would Shakespeare have had Wallenstein express himself!

Goethe's importance for German cultural life lies primarily in the fact that the Frankfurt burgher, on the strength of intellectual gifts, succeeds in becoming Minister and friend of a prince. Then there is his crossing of the boundary between poetry and science. In poetry, however, it is only in the lyric that he is a genius of a unique order.

Monologues are justified only when the speaker makes a statement that he would never confide to others. Schiller has his heroes express in monologue thoughts which they could also very well impart to intimate friends. Man says to himself only what he cannot say to others.

Shakespeare's monologue in *Richard III* is something that Richard could say to no one outside the theater public. More prologue than monologue. It would best be spoken before a closed curtain.

Schiller's declamation is at times terribly banal, as when Wallenstein's daughter laments the death of her beloved friend and concludes with the line: "That is the fate of the beautiful on the earth."

Who was Wornum, the Englishman who, earlier than the German scholars, recognized the spuriousness of the Dresden Holbein Madonna? Surely a dilettante.[2]

The Jews: the people of The Book, as Thomas Mann has Goethe say. The scholars: the people of the books. No wonder that learned Jews are such indefatigable readers, like R. L. Mayer, Panofsky, and others.

The child is both friendly and cruel; the friendliness it outgrows. (Have read this somewhere formulated differently.)

The authors who set out to say something that no one has said before—a difficult task, considering the millions of books that have been written—are to be regarded with mistrust. With the choice of saying something accurate, what they consider accurate, or of saying something that has not yet occurred to anyone, they will always choose the second. Thus particularly Chesterton, but also Nietzsche and Shaw. Therefore a phenomenon of the times. Schopenhauer was still free from this tendency. He is full of wit in order to make something pictorially clear, but never at the cost of veracity.

After a great deal of intellect has been at work, the exact truth appears necessarily banal, and intelligent minds avoid it.

"She speaks without saying anything." A lady of my acquaintance.

36

If P.[3] were a bridge, I should prefer to swim.

Whoever wants to get along with his fellow men should never forget that each one, whatever else he is, considers himself the center of the world. Not so much what he thinks and says, but what he feels, the will and instinct that determine his actions, are egocentric.

"Tact" is the capacity to take into consideration the egoism of others, to reckon with it.

Like someone who never attended a university, he has unbounded respect for learning.

"Faith shall move mountains."—I have never seen mountains moved through faith, but rather mountains bored through by understanding.

This is opposed to Klages and the aversion, become popular, toward intellect, cultural progress, and enlightenment.

With many writers banality begins wherever incomprehensibility leaves off.

This occurs to me in reading a book by Griesebach on Jacob Burckhardt.

In present-day Germany the professors look like mercenaries; in Holland the tram conductors look like professors.

Schopenhauer's aesthetic can be expressed briefly as: "Everything that does not cause pain is beautiful."

Justi, in *Winckelmann I,* remarkable passage:[4] The observation on Impressionism and what follows it is prophetic. Justi (*W. II*) : in front of art works newly come to light the mind is virginal.

A painter does not have the possibility, like a poet or writer in the publication of his "collected works," to leave out and to disown productions he considers unworthy of him. Goethe could do it, Dürer could not. Perhaps Dürer would not have included the Basel illustrations in his collected works.

Riemer as "doppelgänger" of Goethe.

One should not shy at half truths; two half truths, which seem to contradict each other, now and then yield a whole.

In the criticism of style, a distinction is made between intuition and learned, rationalistic research. But it is hard to ascertain how much intuition is concealed in the learned research, and how much knowledge is inherent in the intuition.

The most recent German endeavor of the scholars: they write profoundly, since they have no opportunity any more, likewise no peace of mind, to work scientifically. The "Great Epoch" requires that they conceive "great thoughts." Result: unreadability. This after a look into the *Festschrift* for Worringer (which appeared in 1943 in Königsberg).[5]

Scholars are satisfied when they themselves understand what they have written; they do not think of the reader.

The German scholars fence in their field of thought with the barbed wire of their language, so that no one can penetrate into the field and see how barren it is.

By the way, in recent times there is more of a frivolous journalese, with much questionable imagery. Along with the ambition for depth has come the ambition for wittiness.

The English writers are distinguished from one another by individual ideas and thoughts, not by personal manner of speaking, like the Germans. Uniformly common culture of the English.

Goethe commends the English authors to Eckermann.

The language is so riddled with imagery that only the seeing author can employ it felicitously. Most authors, especially the scholars, do not see. Artists and art connoisseurs ought to write better than, say, jurists or philologists, because they are accustomed to seeing. Now and then this advantage is noticeable, but only now and then.

When someone has died he is mourned and lamented as if something precious had been lost, even though while he lived his existence and his lot were by no means regarded as a source of pleasure or happiness. This contradiction may be explained by saying that in the one case "will" serves the life impulse as a measuring rod, in the other case the intellect. The intellect judges pessimistically on the life which, however, as we feel in sympathy, has the "will" not to give up.

A pair of parents can have two sons, of whom the one is a saint, the other a scoundrel. How senseless, therefore, to try to identify the moral character of a people, of a race, or to think one can do so.

He reminds one of Demosthenes, not because of his eloquence, to be sure, but because of his speech impediment.

Dürer's "Apocalypse" bears the same relation to Luther's coming on the scene as the French Revolution to the appearance of Napoleon.

He expects so little of men, that he does not come to the point of despising anyone at all. He has such slight regard for all, that he does not despise the individual. General contempt for mankind is linked with tolerance for the individual man.

Someone is endeavoring to develop himself from a man to a gentleman.

He who says "no'" appears to stand on a higher level than the yes-man. This superiority may be reached without effort, since to contradict is not more difficult than to conform.—*Written in an album to classmates.*

In an old notebook (1906) I find the following rather nice observation: Everyone with an understanding of art overrates himself in that he seems to himself to excel his professional colleagues; naturally, since he compares, to his own advantage, what they say or write with what he would like to say or write—that is, with what he thinks and feels. Only he forgets that the same goes for the others—that they too feel more than they are able to express.

All painters before Manet saw with one eye, therefore sharply and with objective interest; the so-called Impressionists were the first to see with both eyes, which was not in every respect a step forward. They were no longer interested in perspective construction, which strictly speaking has one-eyed seeing as its hypothesis.

The eye is a phenomenon, a marvel, like a mirror that remembers.

"Much Ado about Nothing"—nice title for many a musical comedy.

Ear and eye: similar connection between physical reception and mental interpretation.

There are no pure sense perceptions.

Without a point of view there is no judgment, with a point of view no generally valid judgment.

Heinrich Mann's political essays appeared in 1935. As opposed to his brother, he has turned out to be right with his radical, unpatriotic, socialistic interpretation.

R. M. Meyer on modern literature. He has read everything, passed judgment on everything. That he could set this task for himself speaks against him.

The same writer's *Nietzsche*. Too-thorough apology. He tortures himself to bring all the contradictions into accord, but does not, in his hero worship, take into consideration the excessive vanity and morbidity of the hero whose wealth of ideas impresses him so forcibly. He speaks a great deal about Nietzsche's inclination to produce an effect. What effect did Nietzsche finally produce? After all, it was exclusively in the realm of language and literature. In the political, the economic, the social fields the effect was harmful, if anything, through misunderstanding of his obscure, pathetic, paradoxical language.

Meyer leaves Nietzsche not a single bad quality.

The "great" men of whom a nation boasts come to be regarded as the representatives of the nation, and with doubtful justice is the nation thereby characterized. For example, Kant on the German spirit. How many have read and understood Kant? His influence is far slighter than is admitted. It is downright comical when a Frenchman, from Kant's information, attempts to comprehend the German spirit. Naturally he cannot read Kant, who in French translation is probably even more incomprehensible than in the original. And if the impossible happens, and he does understand Kant, he still receives a distorted image of Germany. The great men are exceptions—only in defects and weaknesses the representatives of their people. A German trait in Kant is his professorial pedantry.

This after reading Curtius on modern French intellectual life:

> Dies ist ein *amateur marchand:*
> Er sammelt laut und mit *élan,*
> Wenn er sich zum Verkauf bequemt,
> Tut er es leise und verschämt.
> Der wirkliche *marchand* hingegen
> Kauft leise, auf geheimen Wegen,
> Preist das Erworbne laut dann an
> Und bringt es glücklich an den Mann.

> [This is an amateur dealer:
> He collects openly and with élan,
> When he submits to a sale,
> He does so quietly and ashamedly.
> The real dealer, on the other hand,
> Buys quietly, in a covert manner,
> Then recommends the acquisition loudly
> And happily gets rid of it.]

The cleaner a house is kept, the more flecks of dirt fall into it. This applies to aesthetic and literary judgment.

42

"I allow nothing to be given to me," said the thief proudly. (Occasionally to be used figuratively.)

Of rich, but honest parents. (A cheap witticism, but good.)

To utter accurate statements is not so necessary and worthwhile, because they have validity apart from this, or sooner or later gain it. On the other hand, it is useful to make statements in which there is something correct, because relative, partial accuracy easily remains in the dark and unconsidered. The contradiction stirred up by half-right assertions promotes knowledge, since out of Thesis and Antithesis, Synthesis emerges as a new kind of idea.

Have been reading two books by U. Sinclair. Political diatribes against plutocracy, for the workers. All the rich are corrupt, moral principle is only in the poor, or in the rich who renounce the influence of money. Everything is merely negative, destructive, not constructive. How the workers could establish a better order does not become clear.

However, the experience of the Russian experiment is not yet instructive. Presumably autocracy and plutocracy are replaced by an official authority, under which the lot of the workers is not appreciably changed.

Another book of Sinclair's seems to be essentially an auto-biography. One sees here how, in wretched living conditions, he absorbed his venomous hatred for luxury, money, and power. He regards himself a misjudged genius.

According to the proposition: "The steady drop hollows out the stone," Sinclair attacks the power of money, luxury, corruption, while proclaiming in endless variations the same theme: the ideal

43

Konrad Witz,
Holy Family
in a Church
Museo di
Capodimonte,
Naples

sentiment of the have-not, his misery, and the harsh power that is founded on possession.

When a rich man is converted to socialism, there is more proof thereby of the rightness of socialist doctrine than if a poor man, whether consciously or unconsciously, expects an improvement in his own lot from the changed economic system.

K. Witz: "Holy Family in a Church," Naples—perspective and

Basel Cathedral,
interior

appearance not mathematically constructed. To be compared with
a photograph of the Basel Cathedral. The mood of Gothic interior
space is much stronger in the Witz painting. Genius in a certain
sense is more truly receptive than the knowledgeable constructor.
An interior by Manet would resemble the picture by Witz more
than the correct representation would. Unprejudiced view. Witz
was also ingeniously precocious in cast shadows, earlier than the
Dutch.

45

What we perceive does not correspond to the perspective construction—for two reasons. We see with two eyes. The eyes move while seeing. Only if we close one eye and avoid any movement does the impression coincide with the perspective construction.

The picture that is produced through perspective construction does not coincide exactly with our view and that which we see, since we see with two eyes, whereas the perspective construction corresponds only to the one-eyed view.

Here is the reason for the mistrust and the indifference on the part of the Impressionists toward mathematical perspective.

English (also French) writers on art, model aestheticians like Ruskin and Pater, become renowned and are quoted for the sake of their language, as poets, not as scholars. The best Germans (Justi, Burckhardt) become recognized as historians, researchers. Appreciation of language is less to be expected on the part of the English than on the part of the French.

The German art historian who (as a Goethe pupil) was effective as a man of letters, similar to Ruskin or Pater, namely, H. Grimm, is not as revered and quoted as those Englishmen.

Klee's art: visual music. Eye-music.
His images: songs without words. Dynamic ornament.

Profession: bound up with duty, work, pain. A professional art scholar finds it hard to regard works of art, the objects of his study, with enjoyment. Without enjoyment there is no understanding of works of art. This lack I have often observed in colleagues. Genuine love of art is found more in dilettantes and collectors who, as a relaxation from their professions, occupy themselves with art in their leisure hours.

46

Attempt to distinguish the "What" from the "How" in the rendering of a work of art. In every original work the What is in harmony with the How. This is the hallmark of originality. We learn to know the What only in this How. Notwithstanding, the proportion of the What to the How is now thus, now otherwise. In Raphael's "Sistine Madonna" it is different from that in Manet's "Bunch of Asparagus." In the one case what is shown, pictured, brought before the eyes, has meaning of itself, through itself; the How of the pictorial rendering is the means of doing justice to that meaning. The language is on the level of what is to be said. The bunch of asparagus, on the other hand, of itself without significance for mind and soul, becomes through the How, that is, through the way *how* Manet sees, a work of art. The commission that Raphael received required an altar picture, an edifying realization of the Madonna and saints. Manet's bunch of asparagus did not originate because a gourmet wished to look at asparagus. The art lover acquired the picture not because asparagus was to be seen, but rather because he wished to possess a work by Manet's hand. In the cases of Raphael and Manet, the center of gravity lies on the What in the former, on the How in the latter. In a survey of the total of art production, a scale may be formed in which the What, in infinitely many degrees, loses in importance, while the How gains.

The extreme case, which we approach, is wittily characterized by A. Huxley as follows: Without understanding Latin, someone enjoys the tonal color and rhythm of Latin verse.

In the working process in Raphael's case, an obligatory, elevating motivation issued from the task, from the intellectual, the sublime, the human aspect of the theme, whereby the imagination was challenged to create a moving and monumental form. In the case of Manet, on the other hand, the creative passion had no other incentive than the wish to conjure up the vision, the unique visual

Edouard Manet, Bunch of Asparagus
Wallraf-Richartz Museum, Cologne

experience. In the former case the "beautiful," the aesthetically valuable, is created for the glory of the lofty subject; in the other case the "beautiful" is discovered in the visible presentation. An aesthetic purist could perhaps draw the conclusion that the bunch of asparagus is visual art in a narrower sense than the "Sistine Madonna." Raphael's sentiment could, assuming another specific talent, flow into poetry instead of pictorial form, but Manet's sentiment could by no means do so. Visual art has departed further and further from poetry. Less and less do they go parallel ways.

48

Raphael, The Sistine Madonna
Staatliche Kunstsammlungen, Dresden

Instead of making a key for the lock, one must sometimes make a lock for the key, which is harder.

Formerly it was said simply: "Jan van Eyck was a realist." This sounds banal and worthless. Now one says that Van Eyck's art is "objective illusionism," which sounds profound but says ultimately nothing other than that the master was a realist.

In Benesch's obituary of Dvorak (in the Repertorium), Vienna art scholarship shows its megalomania. Claims, challenges, projects of gigantic dimensions.

And how sorry the results.

When, in drawing the profile line of a man's nose, I take in the object with a glance, without looking at the paper, I think I am attaining the utmost in a direct observation of nature. When I sketch the profile of the nose of an acquaintance whom I have not seen for a year—when, as it is awkwardly expressed, I draw "out of my head"—the same degree of truth to nature can, according to circumstances, be reached as by direct observation. This experience ought to show that there is no distinction in kind between the former and the latter action. The time interval, rendered powerless by the tenacity of the memory, which in turn is dependent on the depth of the first impression, is responsible for the distinction in degree.

As it is written today: "The older realistic tendency aiming at the finest tonal gradations has, in Gertrud Staats,[6] who died in 1938, once more confirmed the validity of an unusual force imprisoned in the native environment."

A tendency aims at tonal gradations and confirms the validity of a force!

Figurative language without the capacity to see the image.

"A point of view has expanded." Writers who make use of figurative language without seeing, people who hear but do not see.

When it is hungry, the animal will even kill; man requires no such definite motive.

Racial mixture seems to be good for the intellect. Kant is said to have had Scottish ancestors, Schopenhauer's family stems from Holland, Nietzsche boasts of Polish ancestors, Montaigne's mother was a Spanish Jewess. Spinoza was a Spanish Jew who lived in Holland. Conflict of lineage with environment seems to have a stimulating effect. Jan van Eyck, a Nether-German at a half-French court. Dürer half-Hungarian.

Academicians enter the museum with ideas, art connoisseurs leave it with ideas. The academicians seek what they expect to find, the art connoisseurs find something of which they knew nothing.

The purer the race, the lower the intellectual mobility. Does not, however, apply to the Jews.

Aldous Huxley, "Along the Road" (*The Albatross*, vol. 507), essay on Brueghel.[7] "Most of our mistakes are fundamentally grammatical." (This sentence is from the *Dictionary of Professional Language*, about which I have spoken.) A. Huxley defends P. Brueghel against the charge that for him the interest in content suppressed or diminished the interest in form. Indeed his task was to report human peculiarities. Huxley calls the master "an anthropologist and a social philosopher." I would say: "Judge of men, with a knowledge of his countrymen and contemporaries, poet of tragi-comedies, worldly preacher, humorist." Huxley's

51

sentence about the admirers of pure form is witty: "The process is analogous to reading Latin verses without understanding them—simply for the sake of the rhythmical rumbling of the hexameters." On the whole, the short essay on P. Brueghel is perhaps the best that has been written on the master.

On the subject of Greco, S. Maugham, in *Human Bondage,* is very penetrating.

The obscurity and incomprehensibility of scholarly writing serve as a bulwark of defense. When the obscurity has been cleared up in translating the foreign text into German, there remains either a banality or a questionable, controversial assertion.

In England, men of letters like Ruskin or Pater are famed for their stimulating views on art; in Germany it is historians like Justi or Burckhardt, critics of style like Bode; in France and Belgium it is investigators of old documents.

Some masters are to be appreciated fully by single works, and do not gain in significance by a knowledge of their total production —for example, Terborch. Others are recognized in their full stature only from their entire work. For example, Jan Steen, Dürer, Brueghel, Daumier belong to the second group.

The eye is a mirror, forgetful as a mirror, I have read. The eye is not forgetful, therefore it is no mirror, at least it does not have all the properties of the mirror. It is a mirror connected with an intellectual apparatus, with a storeroom to keep the mirror pictures in place.

Thinking this over, one comprehends that the distinction between drawing or painting from memory and from nature is only one of degree, not a distinction in kind. In all cases is it a question of realizing a preserved, intellectually-assimilated mirror image.

Mental eye, intellectual eye, eye of the mind.

Sight for the sake of vision.

He who takes his own life behaves like an impatient person, like one who cannot wait. Every suicide is untimely.

Art, formerly handmaid in temple and palace, is now mistress in a shabby hut.

Jews have still more aversion to the antique, to classic form, than the Germans. Jewish art historians (Lippmann, Ephrussi, Lehrs, A. Goldschmidt) are for the specifically German. Neumann is for Rembrandt (Burckhardt, on the contrary, for Rubens). According to M. Liebermann there are only two good pictures in Italy, by Van der Goes and Velazquez.

"Love," the erotic inclination passionately directed toward a person, is turned into life from the novel, rather than into the novel from life. At least there is little of it to be observed in life.

Born pessimists become relatively happy in old age, because they have found that not everything was as dark and miserable as they had expected. Born optimists, on the contrary, experience disappointments, so that they, in old age, become relatively unhappy. Both views of the world, pessimism and optimism, are weakened, even refuted, through experience.

Winckelmann, from the Mark Brandenburg, develops the highest enthusiasm for Greek antiquity, and for Mengs, a Saxon, the radical eclectic painter. Innermost longing: the incentive toward

53

a lofty, distant ideal. No Italian was so uncompromising a worshipper of the antique as Winckelmann. Lessing also stemmed from an artistically barren northern district, and sought absolute "beauty" in the most distant and most strange. Want of artistic culture was the preliminary condition without which enthusiasm for the antique could not have mounted so high.

Genius and madness bear the same relationship to each other as tightrope dancing to breaking a leg. The tightrope dancer is exposed to the danger of an accident to a higher degree than one walking on level ground. But not every tightrope dancer meets with an accident, and one cannot recognize the tightrope dancer by the fact that he has broken his foot.

I have written thus already about Van der Goes in my *Altniederländische Malerei*.

I have again read T. Mann's *Lotte in Weimar*. The language is defined by anxious caution and mistrust of the accuracy of the observations. Mann restricts what he says, half retracts it, supplements it with nuances, and the result is a complicated sentence structure. "On the subject of so ambiguous a creature as man one cannot make an unequivocal statement." So similarly he makes excuses, justifies himself. Something of a mannerism, however. Ingeniously interwoven, yet still intelligible. Finesse and some timidity in the observation of psychic incidents. He cannot find satisfaction in analysis. The complicated aspect is looked for everywhere. Mistrust of the simple, the direct, the positive. Many relative sentences. Complexity of the language commensurate with the complexity of the psychical observations. Of course Mann, with poetic sensitivity, has taken pains, and successfully, to affect the language of the beginning of the nineteenth century, the language of Weimar, and that of the pedantic schoolmaster who poetizes in Goethe's atmosphere. And thereby he has indirectly expressed many of his own ideas through Goethe. The loquacious reverence mixed with envy, the vain consciousness of inferiority, are exceedingly refined, and even though too spirited for Riemer, are spirited enough for Mann.

The government not in a condition to give everyone his due gives the same to all.

Much admired and much censured: Picasso.

Since one has no prospect of saying something that someone else has not already said, one takes pains to say it well.

Man kills Time, until Time kills him.

Picasso and companions: madness that speaks melodiously. To simulate depth through opaqueness, meaning through unintelligibility.

As architecture has been call frozen music, the painting of our day can be called music become frozen.
Music for the eyes.

Schopenhauer speaks of "acquired" character. One can also speak of borrowed, feigned, claimed, assumed character. That which is acquired more or less intentionally, and consciously cultivated, is therefore not character, strictly speaking. A stroke of fate can tear off the character mask. Romanstoff: A Jew from a wealthy and respected house has become acquainted, through English books and perhaps also through travelling, with the ideal of the British "gentleman." He succeeds in becoming an English gentleman until loss of money and social position takes away from him the acquired character. Suicide in such a case, or quite different character traits, but emerging from the depths, such as the cautious craftiness of Jewish ancestors. Surely-defined characters are found rather in fiction than in life.

Schiller's characters are as though drawn, those of Shakespeare, painted.

How something happened: imperfect tense. The fact that something has happened: perfect tense.

The imperfect reports on a happening that lies in the past, the perfect states that a happening lies in the past. In the first case the happening is the essential thing, in the second the time relationship of the happening to the present. Since in the second case the time relationship is decisive, the connotation of the negative comes in (not now, now no longer); sometimes the negative is predominant—"I have loved" means "I no longer love." In the imperfect the speaker takes himself into the past, in the perfect he regards the past event from the standpoint of the present. For the imperfect, one can rhetorically substitute the present tense without disturbing the sense. Sometimes in the perfect it is not the negative that is introduced, but the consequence of the happening, the after-effect. In the imperfect the course of the happening is considered, in the perfect, the conclusion. The perfect is sight through the perspective of time. The imperfect is in a higher degree objective; the perfect points to the effect of the happening, to the present. In every statement of the perfect tense something of the present tense is inherent. "He has gained a victory" contains the statement: "He is the victor."

Time-perspective: the thing in space changes according to its distance and position in relation to the eye; the happening, at a distance in time, appears differently to the observer and to the one who experienced it.

The treasure of words belongs to our fathers' heritage, which we must earn in order to possess.

With the imperfect tense we take ourselves into the past; with the perfect we remain in the present, looking at the past.

Example: Where is this picture now? The Berlin Gallery has acquired it. When and how? It was purchased in Paris at a high price.

The X-ray gives to gentlemen who in front of pictures see nothing the possibility of passing judgment on pictures.

The emigrant has the advantage of being able to free himself from the conventions, the prejudices, of his native land, and of being able to remain aloof from the conventions and prejudices of his new country. In a foreign land it is easier to develop one's own individuality, provided it exists.

One can be an emigrant without having left the land of his birth.

The waiter can speak several languages, the writer only one—often not even one.

Have read Brandes' *Caesar*. How could a man of spirit take such pains with this theme? Continual mortal combat. And all from Caesar's own, therefore unobjective, reports and from Cicero's advocatory orations and writings.
Probably events for the most part took a course different from that which Brandes presents with the most pedantic precision.

Virtue often emerges when two vices paralyze each other, compensate each other, such as vanity versus cowardice or versus laziness, avarice versus lust. Vanity in particular is the mother of many virtues.

The wish is father to the thought, its mother is fear. For the optimist the thoughts take more after the father, for the pessimist they take after the mother. How, from such a marriage, is something reasonable to originate?

He who feels himself superior to almost all men receives practice in letting his superiority pass unnoticed, and presents a modest appearance.

To conclude a modest disposition from a modest attitude is a common error.

One thinks perhaps: Somebody cannot paint because he has no talent.
It is not as simple as that.
It is more accurate to say: he cannot paint because his capacity to realize the vision is not sufficient. He cannot paint what he sees. With the same capacity for realization he could, however, hold on to poorer visions.
Therefore the relation between the talent for seeing and the ability to paint is the deciding factor. Thus can someone in his youth produce something good, but afterwards so refine his looking that the hand can no longer keep up with it—he seems to have lost his talent. One can go so far as to assert that someone sees too fine to be able to paint.

When I stand in front of a pillar I know that its boundaries run in a straight line.

When my eye is at a level halfway up the pillar, I must expect, according to the law of perspective, that the lines going up and those going down will approach each other and form an angle.

My vision, however, is quite different—not in accord with the perspective construction.

This is because we do not see out of one point, but in looking move the eye, and furthermore because we see with two eyes. Seeing one part sharply, another appears indistinct. Sight is a combination, a collective view.

The nearer the object to the eyes, the more strongly the evidence of the right eye deviates from that of the left.

This accounts for the fact that the Impressionists no longer showed much interest in perspective construction, lost interest in it.

The chaos presented to the senses is put in order by the mind.

Mannerism is the dregs of a style, sometimes of another's style, occasionally of one's own previous style, as in the case of Cranach.

The old masters saw colored form, the modern ones see shaped color.

In W. Somerset Maugham (*Don Fernando*) I find: "I have long since abjured the heresy prevalent in my youth of art for art's sake. Oscar Wilde popularized it in England and Oscar Wilde learnt it from Whistler." (Probably written about 1930.)

He who "understands" a work of art—as it is expressed in the most comprehensive terms—is, in relation to the one who created the work, a reproducer; his relationship to the producer is similar to that of the actor to the dramatic poet, similar also to that of the pianist to the composer. Painted canvas becomes a work of art only when it produces an effect as a work of art. The beholder, in enjoying it, recreates the work of art, just as the pianist awakens the work of the composer, in that he feels with it, goes with it, lets himself be transported, is sympathetic toward it.

If Goethe's works had not appeared under his name during his lifetime, and scholars had to decide what originated from him and what did not, then would polemics and strife prevail, and certain parts of the works would be attributed to a "doppelgänger." Eckermann or Riemer would come under consideration. Much would be excluded as unworthy. A sharp, clean, but incomplete image of Goethe would result from critical analysis, like the image that Wölfflin offers of Dürer.

One can with some justification speak of workshop production with regard to Goethe's late writings. Goethe directs more than he composes (cf. Hebbel).

Superiority of the English system of government.

Democratic and aristocratic sentiment side by side. The leaders must have distinguished and proved themselves, but need not, as perhaps in France, have risen through stratagem and demagogy. They are more likely half-legitimate; as sons of ruling families they did not attain power through wickedness. British snobbism upholds the aristocratic principle in the democratic system. Chesterton: the English worker says of his fellow-worker that he is a "gentleman."

The woman is particularly suited for sovereignty in a constitutional state. She apparently rules, but is dominated by men (Victoria).

An Englishman from "good" family feels himself considerably elevated when he becomes Minister.

Anti-Semitism has conserved Jewry. I should no longer be a Jew if there had been no anti-Semitism.

Have read Rousseau's *Confessions*. He speaks continually of his stupidity and vices in order to demonstrate how truth-loving he is, moreover how virtuous in that he is clear about his vices, how wise in that his follies have become evident to him.

Heine on Rousseau: He paints himself dark, with the intended effect that the others, the eminent ones, the philosophers, appear still blacker in comparison with him.

Forgeries can be divided into the cowardly and the daring. The daring ones are easier to recognize than the cowardly.

Have read W. Uhde's *Autobiography*, VI, 42, with interest. A typical, extreme case of an art lover in our day. A work of art pleases him only when it displeases others. The satisfaction of being the first, at the time the only, one who scents out the genius, the talent, the soul, is necessary to his enjoyment of art. Moreover, he does not at all enjoy something visible, but rather only his own spiritual and intellectual emotion at his discovery.

A Prussian "corps" student, son of a Posen state attorney, he developed thus in Paris out of rebellious idealism, free from the prejudices of taste. He found agreement on the part of Jews and Americans.

He who takes his own life thinks thereby to make an end, not to begin something new. It is little in keeping with the belief in immortality.

"Let him examine it carefully, who binds himself forever": Advice for couples who enter into "conscience marriages," and other illegitimate alliances.

Boredom was for Schopenhauer a misfortune. However, much that is useful and worthy would not have been created if boredom had not overcome inertia.

A. Under given conditions, namely, in case of evident failure, this "great man" will take his own life.

B. I know him, and I do not believe that. He is cowardly.

A. It may be that you have observed correctly, and that he has now and then shown himself to be cowardly. It is, however, a question not of the degree of his cowardice, but of the proportion between his vanity and his cowardice. Vanity can be so overpowering that cowardice, however strong, cannot prevail against it, so that just as cowardice often makes him cautious, so vanity for once makes him courageous.

In every man there are all the characteristics, but in quantitative relationships that make up the individuality. Circumstances bring to light, expand, heighten, now this, now that, characteristic. Constant characters occur only in literature, especially in the average literature. The great poets have a sense for the instability of character (H. von Kleist, Tolstoy).

Characters are found only in literary creations, character heads only in pictures.

No one is so cowardly that he would not under some circumstances be courageous, and no one so courageous that he would not under some circumstances be cowardly.

Men are stupid, most of them are even so stupid that they do not notice they are stupid.

The first acknowledgment by which a man ceases to be stupid is the insight into his stupidity.

The art scholars who read all day long are like people who study cookbooks and believe that their hunger is thereby satisfied.

Baptized Jews suffer from mild, unbaptized ones from severe, anti-Semitism.

He wrote this in an unguarded hour, of which he had only sixteen daily, since he slept for eight hours.

One can combat his vanity out of vanity—half successfully, but with full success through heightened self-consciousness.

Among the great masters some are like fighters, others like victors. The fighters are perhaps: Michelangelo, Dürer, Rembrandt, Grünewald, Greco, Cézanne; victors: Raphael, Memling, Holbein, Rubens (?)—the historians are more interested in the fighters than in the victors.

In architecture the Gothic is struggle, will, aspiration; the Antique is victory, happiness, repose.

The fighters: those of a melancholy temperament.

Heine (somewhat daring statement): Jews and Germans are spiritually related. In common: aversion to the Classic, to formal beauty in artistic judgment.

The Dane, Jensen, on the subject of the German Jews, quoted by Mann in *Considerations of an Unpolitical Person.*[8]

Professional optimism of the historians.

The state takes money from the citizens in order to pay the officials who collect this money legally and regularly.

Art theory. Painting—drawing.

In the painted work the sea is composed of waves, in the drawing the fence is composed of pickets.

A good metaphor, badly expressed.

Better: in the painted work the parts are related to the whole as waves to the ocean, in the drawing, as the pickets to the fence.

To draw is to know; to paint is to believe. (Quoted under my name. I do not recollect having written it.) *Oh yes,* in the book *Altdorfer.*

The adjective added to the substantive refines—and weakens the concept that the substantive expresses. How strong is the adjective-free noun, for example: "He was a man, take him for all in all." A great, bold, kind man: less effective. Someone has said: "The adjective is the foe of the substantive."

Art theory. The bad painters are the ones who consider reality prosaic in contrast to that which is invented. (Or freely after G. Keller, who says something similar about poets, in *Der grüne Heinrich*.[9]

Referring to Liebermann's definition of *Phantasie.*

Color: the quality of the form.
Form: the quality of the color.

To draw is to measure, to paint is to weigh.

Mankind has become more tolerant, but not so much because it is more discerning, rather because it has become more indifferent and skeptical. The persecution of the Jews in recent times shows that intolerant fanaticism works as effectively as in the Middle Ages, only now it is directed at race, nationality, and social opposites, as it was formerly directed at religion.

64

Proverbs, winged words that come down from anonymous geniuses, are instructive, understandable. Compare Kant's exposition of the categorical imperative with the familiar saying: "Whatsoever ye would that men should do unto you, do ye even so unto them."

What is to be seen is chaos, which we know how to put into order, organize.

Much can be expected from the healing power of custom and relativity.

The "winged words" catalogued by Büchmann are, to be sure, only such as are demonstrable in writings, as quotations that, not so much on account of their sense, as their forceful, pregnant formulation, have penetrated into the general language.

Next to the Bible, Goethe is the chief source of familiar quotations. Goethe has thus become popular contrary to his prediction. His lyric poetry and *Faust*, not his prose, are popular and have provided familiar quotations in great quantity.

One who hears or reads about angels will not so easily doubt their existence as one who sees them in a picture as beings of flesh and blood. The latter aspect is inevitably linked with the thought of growing and dying, and this thought is incompatible with the concept of angels.
The visual arts may have done harm to religious belief.

To be a proletarian is no misfortune. One may be able to observe that rich people are not happier than poor ones. But to become a proletarian is a misfortune, and one which at the present time is befalling many. The worst thing is that demoralization is linked with becoming proletarian. One who is treated unjustly, degraded, and robbed, develops deceit, lies, and hypocrisy in order to save himself. To remain a gentleman without economic security and independence becomes difficult, if not impossible. To become a proletarian means to become a slave.

To be a gentleman without inherited capital is hardly possible, or to remain a gentleman after the loss of capital.

A vain girl of melancholy temperament adopted the habit of laughing in order to show her unusually beautiful teeth—with the result that her temperament brightened. As cheerfulness generates laughter, laughter generates cheerfulness.

The adult is dull in relation to the child. But dull in its original meaning, not mental dullness or stupidity. The senses become blunt, do not remain as receptive and lively as in youth. Insofar as the mind is nourished by the senses, it too becomes lazy. Children are always active or busy, as long as they are not sleeping.

There are two kinds of writers. The first think with the help of words; they are in the majority. A few think in a struggle with words. One recognizes the former in the smooth, flowing style, the latter in the laborious expression.

T. Mann:[10] A writer is a person to whom writing comes harder than to persons in general. Whoever strives to express his own thoughts is like a traveller who is forced to tread unbeaten paths. Words, which he must employ, hold him back, force him to remain on the travelled ways.

The language thinks for us. This is a blessing for the weak, a straitjacket for the strong.

An effort, yes, but for the greatest ones, an effort surmounted.

Transparent depth: a sign is opaque shallowness, with which

depth is simulated, a sign of the reverse. The philosophers, especially the German ones, treasure as a priceless advantage of words that they are incomprehensible.

Nietzsche in his early period, on the subject of Schopenhauer and Wagner, says little about the philosophy of Schopenhauer and little about Wagner's accomplishment. He fluently sketches the ideal of the freely and deeply intellectual men of his time, and reveals his ideal: himself. He projects this ideal on these personalities. For this reason he was able later to see a mistake in such veneration, to leave Schopenhauer behind him and to oppose Wagner. He severs himself not from Wagner, but only from his Wagner-ideal.

In time of distress one comprehends how religion originates, if he does not become actually pious.

That mankind can endure with wars is proved; that it could endure without wars is not and cannot be proved.

The animal world can evidently not endure without war, that is, without a fight for existence.

A state which had succeeded in providing the same living conditions for all citizens—ideal of the Communists—would collapse through the indolence and idleness of the citizens.

The German language is rich, resembling the luxuriant abundance of the forest, while the French is like the clarity of the park or garden. There is a disadvantage and an advantage to the German language. It requires much effort to find one's way in the forest; the French have it easier. Many Frenchmen write well, few

Germans. The German language offers relatively more possibilities, nevertheless it is difficult to master the richness and not become confused by it. It is easier to translate French into German than the reverse.

In the nineteenth century, whereas the art of painting consciously, according to principle and program, sought to become *l'art pour l'art,* the art of fiction took the opposite course, in that it approached science, history, politics, ethics, religion (Tolstoy, Stendhal). Finally, in the twentieth century, U. Sinclair, the complete politician. Compared to Sinclair, Stendhal is an author for a girls' school. "Belles lettres" is no fitting term for the novels which were at their most successful in the nineteenth and twentieth centuries.

The teachers of the Germans in the eighteenth century, Lessing and Winckelmann, were quarrelsome librarians.

The *consensus sapientium* is often nothing but the submissive acquiescence of a flock of sheep. Mistrust has a place when this authority is challenged by scholarly argumentation.

I like to read, but I instinctively avoid reading what others have thought about things on which I myself have formed opinions. I have a positive unwillingness to read something written by others on Netherlandish painting.

On the perfect-imperfect tenses.
Good example: When I lived in Florence I spoke quite good Italian—because I have lived in Florence, I speak passably good Italian.
Imperfect: position in time. Perfect: time relationship. What is past: the cause of what is present.

Foreign word: *desparat*—German: *verzweifelt* (desperate). The foreign word is unearnest, almost ironical, beside the German.

Words that have grown and developed are to be distinguished from words that have been made. For example: *Hose—Beinkleid* (hose-trousers). The made-up words are probably rather recent.

Without a point of view there is no judgment, with a point of view no generally valid judgment.

In a foreign language one says what he can say, not what he wants to say. The more highly the man is endowed, the less he says, even in his mother tongue, what he would like to say. The wise man feels himself in the end sentenced to silence.

Have been reading Mauthner's *History of Atheism,* only the last volume, his critique of language. One who can, with astonishing erudition, write four thick volumes on atheism has not yet freed himself from "faith." Polemic literature can no longer interest a genuine unbeliever.

The "critique of language" is ingenious, hard to understand, and perhaps (I am not sure) it fails in essence. The relation between thinking and speaking, as it seems to me, is falsely conceived.

Ancient art is plastic art. The task predominant in the creative imagination was to represent the gods in human form. The art is for this reason anthropomorphic. Also Christian theism is anthropomorphic. The God who created man after His own, God's image was a sculptor. The man who created the god after his own, man's, image was a sculptor. The mode of seeing of the Antique was that of the sculptor. Vase paintings are projected sculpture. In the Christian Middle Ages painted work was a substitute for relief sculpture. In the urge toward the plastic, the Antique and the Christian met (Michelangelo). The German tribes who were brought into Christianity, if not forced into it, and who did not stand under the constraint of the antique tradition, brought the pictorial outlook, along with the barbaric, into the mode of seeing.

One who regards Nature as that which is created inclines toward sculpture; one who, on the other hand, regards Nature as the creating element inclines toward painting.

The clothed man is more painterly than the naked one. The nude is more the object of sculpture.

Spinoza the contemporary of Rembrandt.

Sculpture and anthropocentric painting are nearsighted, painting which demands space is farsighted.

Venice is somewhat northern (and eastern). Tintoretto is farsighted in spite of his monumentality and cult of the human body (in contrast to Florence).

German art bears the same relation to Italian as the tree to the column. Italians are weak in still life, landscape, portraiture, with the exception of the Venetians, who are half-Italians. In portraiture Raphael is an exception. Landscapists in Italy are Elsheimer, Claude. The best papal portrait: by Velazquez.

Statistics would be interesting on the share of working time scholars spend in reading. I suppose by far the greater portion. They think the thoughts of others who, on their part, have thought

70

the thoughts of still others. This, however, is not thinking in the true sense. Out of boredom and ambition they read critically, that is, contradict. But even this is not thinking in the true sense. The rare, the new, thought occurs only when an individual mind creates it out of impression and contemplation.

Gogol. Have read everything hastily. Development of his psychic life similar to Tolstoy's. At first a sharp observer (neutral, humorous), later a schoolmaster, fanatically religious, despising his poetic activity, transforming it into abstract moralizing. But Gogol was already at the end in his early years and sick both physically and psychically, while Tolstoy was healthy and grew old. Gogol travelled in a short time the distance for which Tolstoy needed much time. Specifically Russian: the strong tension between worldly realism and uncompromising spiritualism. Extreme in both.

In every artistic utterance the factual is to be distinguished from the symbolic, now in this, now in that proportion to one another In poetry there is more symbol value than in prose, in music the effect is pure symbol, in the song the text is factual, the melody, symbol.

The measure of the symbolic content is the deciding factor in the artistic effect. One has to translate Goethe's poems into prose in order to grasp the essence of the poetic effect. The degree of the symbolic is at the same time the degree of the artistic value.

Publications of private collections are the swan songs, or grave monuments, of the collections.

The only art which can (and does) fully meet the demand of *l'art pour l'art* is music. Painting is sovereign in a higher degree than architecture, but in a lesser degree than music.

71

That music is art in itself someone has stated in a not entirely contradictory sense as follows: Only a musical person may understand visual art, may have the sensitiveness for its aesthetic impact. To be sure, music enters the service of the church and of poetry in the song, in the church hymn, in the opera, but it can keep itself free, which painting in modern times is attempting, rather unsuccessfully, to do.

L'art pour l'art for the eye is ultimately only geometric ornament.

To be cautious, to take care of one's self, therefore to take the future into consideration in one's actions, is for better or worse a human characteristic. The animal is not cautious in the true sense. Deep meaning of the language. The animal avoids only dangers that are immediately threatening, but does not guard against them beforehand. To visualize what lies before one at the time. When foresight is strongly developed and combined with farsightedness, it can enable a man, according to temperament and other dispositions, to become either a successful organizer or else a skeptical procrastinator, a shirker, a "gloomy spirit." Foresight, fostered by experience, grows with the years; but it is also fostered by the imagination, therefore also as an inborn characteristic, or one that asserts itself early.

Proust on the subject of Ruskin (quoted by Ernst Robert Curtius). All true criticism begins by ascertaining the formal elements of an author—not his thoughts, not his feelings. Such criticism cannot be learned. For those details on which it depends cannot be sought—they must flash upon one. Critical talent is nothing other than being struck by such individual features. . . . The calm and passivity of pure receptiveness must be the fundamental attitude of the critic. . . . It applies to stylistic criticism in the visual arts. Cited by me in regard to Dürer.

In order to write the second part of *Faust,* it was not enough to

72

be such a genius as Goethe was; he had also to have become so famous and venerated, so "classic," in order to be able to let himself go with such sovereign disdain for standard requirements. How many obscurities, how many absurdly scholarly allusions among witty *aperçus* and lyrical effusions. How many faulty rhymes.

Talleyrand (witticism). He says of a politician that he pretends to be deaf because he can no longer hear that the people are speaking of him.

If Goethe had spoken a purer German, it would have been harder for him to write poetry. His rhymes are often not pure.

Have been reading Wolfe. Prodigiously sharp eye for human weaknesses, prodigious memory for that which he experienced in youth. The father and mother, forcible in a sinister way, intensively portrayed in their manner of speaking. Everything is autobiographical. He is morbid, obsessed, cannot get rid of recollections. Wordy, similar to U. Sinclair, but Wolfe is a poet, Sinclair a politician who employs the form of the novel. The chaotic element in American life, the tension of harsh contrasts, becomes clear. Revolt against the satiated, the civilized.

Have read S. Lewis (*Sam Dodsworth*). America in contrast to Europe very sharply characterized. Describes how a decent, average American in Europe loses his security, his self-respect, in dependence upon his vain, snobbish wife. One-sided, but entertaining.

Have read Flaubert's *Maxims,* taken from his letters. Remarkably pessimistic, skeptical, close to Schopenhauer, un-French. The art of writing was alone important to him, as Schopenhauer found only his thinking important. Everything else was contemptible and worth nothing.

73

When someone declares he is proud to be a Jew, one need not take him literally. The speaker is merely too proud to conceal that he is a Jew, and to allow the notion to occur that he is ashamed of his origin. He wishes to be proud of his origin, and may also make attempts to discover grounds for such pride.

The Jew has the attributes and characteristics of the aristocracy that has come down in the world, rather than those of the proletariat that has come up.

He simulates pride, in order to avert the suspicion that he is assuming shame.

He who cannot say "no" is Everyman's slave (Montaigne?).
By the way, often my failing.

A Vienna wit: "I am proud to be a Jew. If, in fact, I were not proud of it, I would not cease to be a Jew. Therefore I'd rather be proud of it."

He is on friendly terms with many who are not on friendly terms with him (characterization of an acquaintance of mine).

Proust, of whose works I have read nothing, was, according to a wordy, imprecise description by Curtius, a rich, weak-willed, skeptical mind, whose life consisted in the observation of sensuous impressions. His people are like him. Enrichment and impoverishment of observation. To will and to think are without interest to him, almost ruled out.

Nietzsche on the subject of the Jews in *Human, All Too Human,* a very remarkable passage.[11]

Have been reading Kerr again. Vain, snobbish, arrogating importance to himself, applying everything to himself, at the same time witty, ingenious, capable of judgment, fine-nerved more than fine-feeling. He must have provoked a great deal of opposition and aversion. Sets himself up as cavalier, world traveller, gallant.

Spinoza, as quoted by Schopenhauer, said that a stone which is thrown would imagine, if it had consciousness, that it was flying of its own will. I, who am no stone, have on the contrary the feeling that I am being hurled, while I am apparently doing something of my own will. Am I then more rational than the rational stone? Of course the stone has read neither Spinoza nor Schopenhauer.

When Schopenhauer lets moral principle rest on sympathy, he has ultimately based it upon egoism, since the one who acts altruistically out of sympathy is thereby freed from a sorrow with which the suffering fellow man has infected him. By the way, a very firm foundation.

The "great man": a public misfortune. The organic development of mankind is interrupted, arrested, by the encroachment of demoniacal passion for power (Luther, Frederick II, Napoleon). If one remains free from hero worship, then the suffering, the misery, the disaster will be measured as consequences of the seizure of power—disaster that has no relation to the achievements. Without Luther, Frederick II, and Bismarck, Germany would slowly have become organically unified and strong from natural sources of power. As for Luther's action, this may already have been noted. The notion that the "great man" can contribute much to promote development is an over-estimation of individual insight and foresight.

"Men make history," but only the history that exists in the schoolbooks, not the essential history of mankind.

Talleyrand: more shrewd than Voltaire, than Bonaparte . . . than *tout le monde*.

National vanity produces a pernicious hero cult, but on the other hand transfers the achievements of individuals to "the genius of its people."

75

The "great man" thinks, after something has happened, that he willed it.

Moral principle as a mainspring of action is more effective indirectly than directly. Man judges as a moralist. John is regarded by Paul as a sinner or as a man of honor, and so also does every people present itself to every other people. For this reason John is induced, out of ambition or vanity, to prove himself, or at least show himself as a man of honor. The concept of honor, passion for fame, esteem, are cultivated with respect to the moral judgment of fellow men. To be sure, cynical doubt should not go too far. Custom, religion, rearing, teaching, inherited concepts, lend aid to the indirect working of the ethical impulses and thus produce something like a positive morality.

Man judges so severely as a moralist because he seeks to protect himself against dangerous neighbors. In political life the weak peoples pay particular attention to the sinfulness of the menacing strong ones. Morality based on egoism and therefore securely grounded. Morality as a heritage is difficult to demonstrate. The child is amoral. Morality in animals remains to be investigated. Only the dependent domestic animals develop morality (canine fidelity).

Nietzsche recommends Eckermann's *Conversations with Goethe* as the best German book (or something like it). It is remarkable that he has taken no exception to the fact that a genius preserves so much sound common sense. One would have supposed that so moderate and conciliatory a mentality would not have appealed to him at all. The sober clarity, pedantic objectivity of the aged Goethe does not at all seem to suit Nietzsche's intellectual extremism and psychic morbidity. After all, when did Nietzsche recommend the book? He was for some time an "enlightener." [12]

When a political catastrophe has reached its climax, men think of fate, of the inevitable happening, no longer of individual responsible persons. They have the feeling that to have set this in motion surpasses human power. Accordingly the leaders lose in importance, and blame is meted out to them in a lesser degree. When a war is ended in a short time, glory falls to the victor, blame to the vanquished, but when the war lasts, stretches out, it is felt to be like a catastrophe of nature from which there is no deliverance, and for which no one is to blame.

Schopenhauer: athlete of the brain. Nietzsche: acrobat of the brain.

In the newspaper literature of these days desirable conditions are described and untruthfully published as if they existed.

Tall men must stoop, because the doors in city and country are scaled to medium size, or they knock their heads severely.

Winckelmann's influence shows how far a heedless enthusiast, little capable of judgment, can go. His enthusiasm for a dreamed-of art was incited by an abnormal disposition. Archaeology builds upon his capacity for inspiration, his mania.

Stefan Zweig was a cultivated, enthusiastic, grateful mediator of spiritual values, optimistic, deeply disturbed by war, nationalism, incitement of peoples. He is said to have taken his life in South America in 1942 or 43.[13] This is very plausible. He was not equal to the Second World War. (After reading a collection of Zweig's essays and discourses).

The teachers of Germany were schoolmasters, librarians, pedants, unperceptive and arrogant in their ideas, quarrelsome—Lessing, Winckelmann, Kant (Goethe excepted, but his influence came late). Schopenhauer would have gone farther had he not started from

Kant. His criticism of Kant was more fruitful than his veneration of Kant. Nietzsche was the first to free himself entirely from Kant.

One who, like H., takes away from the Jews possessions, power, the possibility of acquiring property, at the same time annihilates anti-Semitism, which depends above all upon ill-will, envy, and fear of superiority. Signs of this effect were to be noted in 1941.

T. Mann in *Lotte in Weimar* has Goethe express some remarkable statements about Jews, Germans, emigrants. Actually the statements are Mann's (not Goethe's).

According to Schopenhauer the power of will, the character, is inherited from the father, the intelligence from the mother. If this were so, ideal results would have to be produced by the marriage of a Prussian officer and a Jewish girl. That it is so is hardly to be proved. Bismarck once recommended such a racial mixture.[14]

Nietzsche in his middle period offers a remarkably objective judgment on the Jews, somewhat in the spirit of contradiction, however.[15]

Schopenhauer, like Hebbel, both of whom occasionally express themselves in an unfriendly fashion concerning the Jews, were in need of the Jews as mediators between themselves and their contemporaries.
Jews: agents even in immaterial things.

Have been reading Curtius on modern French literature, on Proust. It is striking how the English—not the Germans—ally themselves with the French mentality. Germany is as though ruled out.

Decisive cultural changes are to be traced earliest of all in works of art. So says Curtius. This applies to Dürer's "Apocalypse" as a premonition of the Reformation.

Albrecht Dürer, The Riders of the Four Horses. Woodcut from the
Apocalypse

The Metropolitan Museum of Art, Gift of Junius S. Morgan, 1919

Once the system exists, the windows of observation tend to close. So says C. Justi, *Winckelmann III,* p. 89, in opposition to academic art scholarship.[16]

Power in itself is bad. In order to attain to power, wickedness is necessary. Among the wielders of power, therefore, only the inheritors of power, that is, the legitimate princes, are possibly well-disposed and benevolent, not the usurpers, dictators, presidents. He who has gained power through his own strength is the superior opponent of the lawful ruler. The legitimate ones are, with exceptions, relatively weak. And so the unfortunate common people have only the choice between weak leaders, perhaps well-disposed, or strong, wicked ones. If the legitimate ruler is strong, then he is not well-disposed; all the same, he feels himself more secure, requires less force or stratagem in order to hold on to his power than does the dictator.

In England the sons from "good" families find it relatively easy to come to power; they hardly have need of intrigue or striving. Besides, they are at the summit, even without office and public position.

Words of the vernacular, however hackneyed, can again and again produce a moving effect. *"Mütter"* in Goethe, "man" in Shakespeare ("He was a man"). Foreign words are *Wörter,* words of the vernacular are *Worte.* A vernacular word is painterly, with undefined boundaries; a foreign word is sharply defined, like a drawing. "Terminus": a limited concept.

The scholarship of the Middle Ages not in the vernacular had both an advantage and a disadvantage. Misunderstanding was less possible.

The intellectually distinguished man is like an abnormally tall man who, in order not to strike his head, must duck and make himself small. Those who believe in themselves often do not think that others believe in them. For that reason they present an insecure appearance, in spite of great self-respect.

Everyone is of the opinion that he has sufficient intelligence, for the simple reason that he feels the lack of, and tests, his intelligence with his own intelligence. Since, however, he observes more accomplishment, more success of intellect, in others than in himself, he attributes that superiority to every possible privilege and beneficial circumstance, in order not to have to acknowledge a greater degree of intelligence. So he praises diligence in the others, blames their perseverance, ascertains lucky circumstances.

When someone praises another as clever, he at the same time establishes the fact that, were he not just as clever, that quality would not have revealed itself to him. "How clever I must be, if I have perceived that cleverness": that is his unexpressed thought. On this happy delusion subsist the historians, critics, and literati who write books or essays on great minds (S. Zweig, for example).

What old age wishes for itself, youth has in abundance. And vice versa.

The fish thinks the innocent hook has designs on it; of the hostile angler it knows nothing.

In the Gospels, Christ is indistinctly and inconsequently proclaimed as the Son of God. Through Joseph He is descended from David. Therefore King of the Jews. In contradiction to this: begotten by the Holy Ghost. Much in the life of Christ does not fit into the concept of His divine nature. It was the Roman Church, with the Trinity and the Immaculate Conception, that first firmly circumscribed the orthodox dogma, and doubtless for that reason did not wish the congregation to read the Gospels.

81

With the invention of book printing, the way was prepared for the Reformation, and indirectly for the dissolution of Christian doctrine.

The self, which one is most acquainted with, one knows the least. The material for observation is too large to be able to be caught in the net of the concepts. The observations contradict one another. All self-portraits are literary, false, and not only because objectivity is lacking.

Goethe has humor, Schiller has not. Goethe is witty without intending to be; Schiller is witty knowingly and intentionally.

Humor feels what is laughable, wit recognizes it.

Dostoevski has humor, Tolstoy has not (I read this in an English essay).

Only the one who has little knowledge about something believes that he knows it.

In the self-portrait, "will" forces itself more into the view than in other portraits.

When someone finds nothing else he can be proud of, he finds a reason to be proud in referring to the land of his birth, the place of his birth, or his age.

Referring to the policy of the present government. Instead of giving to each one his due, it gives the same to all.

The world is so untruthful, so accustomed to lying, that the truth sounds unbelievable.

Frederick II wrote the *Anti-Machiavelli* in the spirit of the Florentine, before he employed the methods of the master.

There may have existed, or at least there could have existed, significant literature which does not exist. An author who was in advance of his time could not count upon understanding and acceptance, therefore found no publisher. Only books whose authors think and feel in some degree in accord with their time, at least with a minority of their contemporaries, come to light. Thus Stendhal, had he been born forty years earlier, would not have found publication, and U. Sinclair just as little. Thoughts which were expressed for the first time about 1900 could have stirred much earlier, provided someone—even in a monologue—dared to utter them. From this it is to be concluded that the freest and greatest minds may not have found expression in words.

Jewry has benefited by the fact that it was driven out of lands which were on the verge of downfall, and escaped to lands which had a future (Spain, Holland, Germany, America). Hatred of the Jews: symptom of sick, inwardly-weak peoples (autocratic Russia, Germany under dictatorship).

When a people feels itself unfortunate, it sees in the Jew the enemy which caused the misfortune.

Conversation between an old and a young art lover:

The old one: The pictures which you admire, my young friend, are nevertheless nothing but vain attempts to imitate nature. The great masters recognize, or at least suspect, the fruitlessness of their endeavor, and therein lies the tragedy of their fate.

The young one: But, master, how is it then to be explained that the pictures are sought after by art lovers, and afford pleasure?

The old one: This is because the art lovers see still worse than the painters. As soon as they have learned to see well, they have no more need of the art, and look upon man's work with some contempt.

The young one: What you say, I can apply only to the "naturalists." There is, after all, also a personal artistic form of expression.

The old one: Is there really? Is not the "artistic form" in the end nothing but an evasion? The painter makes a virtue of necessity, out of his inability he makes his style, out of an unconscious style a conscious manner. The great ones were and are subjectively all naturalists and unfortunate lovers of nature.

We can view the moon calmly and measure its boundaries, but not, on the other hand, the sun. The moon bears the same relation to the sun as talent to genius.

Monotheism, like polytheism, inclines toward sculpture, pantheism toward painting (Spinoza—Rembrandt). God, who created Adam, was a sculptor, and the man who created God after his own image was a sculptor. The man who traced the divine in all things was a painter.

"The portrait painter seeks the moment when the model looks most like himself; in the capacity to find and hold this moment lies also the talent of the portraitist . . ."

Dostoevski, *Tagebuch eines Schriftstellers,* pp. 143-44, I (1873), published by A. Eliasberg. (In the same book are remarks on genre and on history and Bible pictures, pp. 144-45).

The successful forger would have the capacity to realize a vision, only he has no vision, that is, no original vision of his own. His relation to the artist is, literally, like that of the actor to the poet.

The "What" of a communication can be translated into another language, but not the "How."

Van Gogh: a genius without talent.

What Goethe says to Eckermann about Schiller well applies to Dürer. Schiller was an extraordinarily gifted person who tormented himself with philosophical thinking that could in no way help him. It was not Schiller's way to act with a certain unconsciousness and, as it were, instinctiveness—rather he had to reflect on everything he did. . . .

If one substitutes humanistic learning and theory for philosophy, it all applies to Dürer. Goethe says also that Schiller valued the idea more highly than all nature, and thereby nullified nature.

Pirckheimer was for Dürer what Kant was for Schiller (*Eckermann I*, p. 84). But Dürer at times comes closer to Goethe than to Schiller. See the passages in which Goethe speaks of his visual memory (also to Eckermann).

Both passages are quoted in my Dürer essay.

The academic scholars who approach works of art by way of ideas are taking pains to make a lock for their key, instead of a key for a lock. When the key, namely the preconceived idea, does not fit into the lock, it does not open, and they manipulate the lock, that is, the work of art, by force. Thus have Schmarsow and Beenken worked over the Ghent Altar.[17]

Eckermann to Goethe: "Then you apparently wish to point out that the more one knows, the more poorly one observes?" "By all means," answered Goethe, "when the transmitted knowledge is bound up with errors."—The critics of style, whose knowledge is always connected with erroneous ideas, ought to think about this.

One must be able to thaw out frozen concepts.

Cézanne is supposed to have said that he was the only painter in Europe. This was his conviction, and anything but vanity, ambition, or self-praise. He was, in fact, not at all satisfied with his accomplishments. A natural feeling of the creative painter; indeed one could assert that an original painter, in the strictest sense, is only that one who regards himself as unique, since he considers only his own vision accurate, and that of the others false. Cézanne was honest enough not to express himself modestly.

Laws of development.

Is there a generally valid rule for the intellectual and spiritual development of man? If so, a significant means of classification of stylistic criticism would thereby be gained. It is not to be expected that one would dare go so far as to say: this is the work of a young man, that the work of an old one.

The style of the period, all possible influencing factors, individual tendency, perhaps make the performance of a twenty-year-old appear like that of an old man. One can sooner venture, in front of two works by the same master, to determine that this one was done before that. For the chronological arrangement of undoubted works, a generally valid rule may be serviceable. In many cases there are obstacles, as, for example, when the master died early and was not able to develop organically, or when the series of works is incompletely preserved.

Engravings confirmed by a signature, and which are preserved almost without a gap over a long period of production, allow one most easily to observe the rule. To be sure, it is also in such favorable cases that one must think of the forces which counteract the organic development. It is to be expected, from a knowledge of human nature, of the growing, thriving, and dying away of the physical and psychical organs, that in youth the receptiveness, eagerness to learn, curiosity, force of will, instinctive impulse, are relatively great, while circumspection, experience, self-restraint, are lacking. The artist in particular is driven, by the multiplicity of visual experiences, to restless, rash, and impatient boldness. This applies to the strong, original talents; the average ones will begin by imitating, will keep to the rules they have been taught.

86

In youth a realist, especially regarding details. To come piecemeal close to nature is the goal. Capacity for change, fluctuation of quality. In the course of time the intellect mounts, while force of will, naiveté, instinctive action diminish. Criticism, judgment on the result. The law of inertia prevails more and more, especially in case the creation is attended by success. Production becomes uniform, routine, growing out of visual practice, and less out of stimulating visual experience. The mature master believes he knows what he wants to do and what he can do. The ambitious one repeats what has brought him success.

If, with the prejudices as to the normal development of the physical and psychical organs, one examines the masters' biographies which are the best from the point of view of confirmed life-dates and preserved works, such as the biographies of Dürer, Raphael, and Rembrandt, one finds first of all no confirmation, no prevalence of the law of nature. But it remains profitable and productive to work with that scheme, to apply that measuring rod, and to ask in each case which forces worked against the natural development on account of character, living conditions, teaching, or taste of the period. For example, Van Dyck died in the prime of life, but his last pictures have something senile about them; Dürer in early youth is self-satisfied, evidently accomplished, untroubled; his earnest endeavor is aroused when he is twenty-six years old. The reason: apprenticeship, surroundings, South German production of about 1490—he dominates them. Everything is easy for him. What is required in the Nuremberg workshop he performs without effort. In Basel and Strasbourg about 1493 he surpasses his comrades. Then Venice. Here for the first time are higher demands, a feeling of imperfection, smallness. Ambition awakes. Lucas van Leyden: the greatest contrast. At his strongest in naive youth. Increasing experience is harmful for him, while intellect at first heightens Dürer's powers, later harms them. Each talent has a definite measure of the power of expansion, but in the one it is dissipated early, in the other it endures.

The development of the physical organs is most easily subjected to a generally valid law. Youth is vigorously awkward, manhood is vigorously adroit, old age shows a weakened vitality. The eye becomes farsighted.

The growing farsightedness of the great, the original, masters is to be observed with regularity (Rubens, Rembrandt, Titian). It has the effect of an increasingly large scale, a dearth of detail, an encompassing view. Where this does not become evident, the question to be asked is, why not? Why not in Altdorfer's work, in Cranach's? The answer is, the pressure of the taste of the period, to which average talents in particular defer.

"Il y a une immense différence entre voir une chose sans le crayon dans la main, et la voir en la dessinant." Paul Valéry, *Degas Danse Dessin,* Paris, Gallimard, 1938. The phrase is probably from Degas himself.

While the painter imagines he is looking at nature, he is already looking at a picture, his picture.

Much reading can now no longer hurt me, because I no longer retain anything in my memory. Reading is merely a temporary diversion.

Ethically Dürer was on Luther's side; as a citizen he turned against the excesses which were consequences of Luther's action. In the former as well as the latter attitude he is German. Not the theological controversy, but rather the German morality led him to the Reformer.

T. Mann in *Considerations of an Unpolitical Person,* on the subject of Expressionism.[18]

Conscious departure from reality (Picasso), "non-art," folly. I have similarly explained that we only come to an understanding with the personal vision of the images because the vision has come out of the reality familiar to us.

[Distinction between the German words *Gesicht* and *Vision*]

Gesicht—plural: *Gesichte*—what is seen, what has been seen, not what is to be seen. *Vision* is not exactly the same, because by that term it is emphasized that the spiritual eye sees something which the corporeal eye has not seen. A mirror image: what is to be seen. Therefore there are three steps: 1) mirror image, pure visual statement of the object (which, strictly speaking, does not exist); 2) *Gesicht,* subjectively assimilated mirror image; 3) *Vision,* subjectively fashioned image—to be sure, from recollection of mirror images. Recollection of art not one's own, as well as the experience of realization by this or that technical means, contributes to *Gesicht,* still more to *Vision.* Whoever draws or paints, who has seen Manet, sees, and is thereby guided, either thus or otherwise.

Dante, when asked "Who recognizes the Good?" answered "He who recognizes the Bad." (Thus according to Schopenhauer). This is also to be borne in mind in art judgment. One ought to ask, in front of imitations and copies: "What is the underlying reason that the effect is missing?" Thereby one learns upon what the effect rests.

Impressionists avoid banality in that they see unsharply.

Language is not only deep in meaning, but sometimes malicious. "I believe in . . ." that is to say "I do not have exact knowledge." God: believable, credible.

It is the Dutch above all who made something "out of" that which is presented to the corporeal eye, and the something they made out of it consists of drawings and paintings.

The Flemings and the Italians did not make quite so much out of it, for the reason that in creating a visual image they were not satisfied with what is presented, but took it as a starting point of the formulation, in composing, stylizing, idealizing.

How deep in meaning is language. The Netherlanders, Germans, and English speak of "still life," the French of *"nature morte."* The outlook on the world revealed in the former term is that life, even though seen as still, that is, immobile, is pantheistic in feeling, in the latter that it is nature, to be sure, but seen dead. The Dutch would perhaps speak of dead nature in referring to the spoils of the hunt, but never in the case of flowers and fruits. For the Latins man alone is "living." Sculpture, which can have nothing to do with dead things, is predominant. If one chooses the greatest painters of still life, one encounters Kalf, Beyeren, Chardin, Manet, Cézanne. No Italian, no German, no Englishman, no Spaniard. (Manet, Cézanne: painters in the strictest sense.) Germans are not still-life painters, because of a pretentious intellectuality, and because they are more draughtsmen than painters; Italians are not, because their imagination is anthropomorphic; the English are not, because the taste of their exclusive society is more aristocratic than bourgeois; the Spanish are not, because of their pessimistic outlook on the world, stemming from the Christian religion.

After the public has noticed that it makes itself ridiculous by praising what it likes, it keeps silent, or pretends to praise things it dislikes.

Before the invention of photography, the painters had two problems: to record and to compose. Since now photography records better, the artists think they ought to limit themselves to composition. One sees what comes of that.

Picasso could say—perhaps has said: "Before the invention of

90

photography, the painters were photographers." I myself, who do not share Picasso's point of view, have had the notion, in front of Potter's "Bull" in The Hague: "This animal has let itself be photographed."

What the artist experiences in looking is partly passive sense perception, partly active intellectual forming—choosing, omitting, capturing this, but not that, with his glance. In the active capturing, one can distinguish a conscious from an unconscious attitude, and come to the opinion that unconscious action leads to style, conscious action, on the contrary, to mannerism. Of course, consciousness, thought, what we know of things, association of ideas, are never to be ruled out completely, but can recede in proportion to the surrender to the feelings. In any case, even if one clings to the antithesis of style and manner in the sense indicated, one may detect in every style, therefore personal imprint, something more or less of mannerism, therefore conscious, intentional formulation. For conscious and unconscious in the sense that I have employed these concepts here, one may employ the antithetical concepts "soul" and "mind," which have become popular in recent times. One could accordingly state it thus: the art form, insofar as it springs from the soul, is to be designated as style, insofar as it issues from the mind, as manner.

As someone with a net catches fish, but not the water, so the net of the concepts grasps the typical, but not the individual. Every characterization classifies the individuality into a type. The concepts are a net, not a bucket. Truth slips through the meshes of the net of the concepts.

Hebbel, *Tagebuch* III, p. 292:
. . . infallible criterion for genius and talent . . . that one asks

91

himself, when confronted with an impressive performance, whether or not, were his own ability raised to a high enough potential, he himself would have been capable of it. If he dares to answer the question affirmatively, he finds in himself a thread which, duly spun out, has itself joined to the other. In this case one is always dealing with a talent, and only in the opposite case with the genius. . . . The most ordinary poet . . . would achieve a poem like Schiller's "Glocke" if his power were strengthened a million times, but Schiller himself would never produce an "Erlkönig."—Similar to my definition in the unedited book (p. 129).

We are a match for talent, at least through the capacity for receptiveness, not performance, but for genius not even through the capacity for receptiveness. (So, approximately, says Schopenhauer). Not completely pertinent. Even if this is true, genius remains totally incomprehensible.

If not the intellect, at least the feelings can approach genius.

The scholar "searches." Essentially his activity consists in searching. He always wants to find something. It makes a decisive difference, however, whether one knows, while searching, what he wishes and expects to find, as when one looks for strawberries in the woods, or whether in the search one is surprised at what he finds. The researchers can be divided into those who look for strawberries, and those who are curious as to how that which they may perhaps find will look. To the first class belong the academicians, to the second the dilettantes who strive for connoisseurship.

Even the architect makes do with the ruler, the yardstick, and the compass. Observation of Frank Harris, the Irish writer, who was no professional in art matters, but was a keen observer with a versatile mind. He measures the intervals of the columns of the Parthenon and finds them unequal (thus in the German edition of the *Autobiography*).

Form = place of the color.

Color = the "How" of the form.

Form = the "Where" of the color.

Locality, quantity of the appearance: form.

Quality of the appearance: color.

For one musically gifted it is just as difficult to sing a false note as for an ungifted person to sing a true one.

I cannot afford to lie. My memory is not good enough.

I cannot believe that a deaf expert can give a certificate of opinion; he does not hear which author's name he has written down.

An artist of high rank and original talent will not appreciate the results of his pains, nor, to be sure, those of others. The painter in particular will regard the rendering of nature as nothing but a vain attempt. When an artist presents a conceited and self-satisfied appearance, this speaks against his talent, unless he is pretending, playing the "great man."

The visions of the painters are more beautiful than their paintings.

The art lover can perhaps go so far as to share the visions of the artists. And then he can give up their pictures, which after all are less perfect than their visions.

When we have learned from the painters how to see, we no longer need their pictures, since we, in looking at nature, create our own pictures—of course, only for ourselves.

The artist loves nature, not his art. The art is loved particularly by dilettantes and amateurs.

Libraries: cemeteries of the minds.

Reminiscences

Lippmann

Before I came into contact with Bode (right after I had concluded my university studies), I entered the Print Room as a volunteer and came under the jurisdiction of F. Lippmann. After the year as volunteer I remained as voluntary secretary in Lippmann's entourage. He had attained the post of Director at an early age, perhaps mainly through the favor of the Empress Frederick, at that time Crown Princess. Lippmann made a rather foreign impression among the Prussian officials. Prague, Vienna, and London had stamped him with a man-of-the-world air. He was indolent, epicurean, well-to-do through his marriage with a German-Jewish-English wife, a collector and householder. Somewhat irregularly educated, but with a strong intuition for artistic values, he concentrated broadly upon the essentials and accomplished great things for the Berlin collections. He was more of an organizer than Bode, and understood how to make others do good work. A little after the English pattern—he was strongly English-oriented—he arranged the Print Room in an excellent manner, with much understanding of the technical and practical side. His publications also (*Dürer Drawings,* International Chalcographical Society) bear witness to his taste and his sweeping initiative. Coming from a rich family which was ruined in the '70's, he had in his early years successfully collected pictures, with a precocious understanding of the Early German School. This first collection of his passed into the possession of Hermann Goldschmidt in Brussels, and was later auctioned at Müller's in Amsterdam. In Vienna and in London, Lippmann came into contact with museum life. After his marriage and in a secure position, he once more formed a collection in Berlin, acquiring Early Netherlandish and Early German paintings at a time when these things were not yet highly appreciated. Among Berlin art lovers R. von Kaufmann was one competitor to be taken seriously. Even Bode, at least in the early period, rather neglected that field. My interest in the German art of the sixteenth century—my doctoral dissertation was on Altdorfer—enabled me to gain Lippmann's favor. And I imagine I owe it to Lippmann's good opinion of my capacities that without any effort on my part, Bode called me to assist him. I call attention to the circumstance that, in Berlin at least, it was the Jews who began to occupy themselves with German art as researchers and collectors—R. von Kaufmann, Lippmann, A. Goldschmidt—while the art-loving "Aryans" turned their interest predominantly to the Italian Renaissance, like Von Beckerath. This situation stands in contradiction to the biased, nationalistic boasting that has recently become prevalent. Lippmann was intelligent to the limit of shrewdness, and now and then rather odd. When his only son, who was for a time a successful art dealer, developed a serious abnormality, it may have been the germ of a morbid tendency already present in the father. Lippmann fell ill suddenly of a heart ailment; the robust man did not attain the advanced age of Bode, who was afflicted by illness all his life.

I owe a great deal to the masters of connoisseurship, Bayersdorfer, later Scheibler, Lippmann, and Bode—far more than to the university professors A. Springer, Schmarsow, and Von Brunn. I have always felt the lack of a strictly scientific foundation, but have consoled myself with the observation that in the field of art not much is to be attained by scholarship. Indifferent and inattentive in school, finishing the university with impatient haste in six semesters, then directly and almost without pause obligated to the practice of museum service, I never found time for persevering work, nor could I fill in the gaps in my education. I also look back with regret upon my many travels. Official trips and journeys on a tightly scheduled leave of absence. Everything flew past me too quickly and left no deep traces behind. I was and am indolent, even though industrious and conscientious as soon as an obligation presses me. I must say I am astonished at the relatively large quantity of my productions as a writer, but I maintain that the stimulus to write almost always came to me from the outside. Thus I undertook the writing of the fourteen volumes of the *Altniederländische Malerei* at the urging of Paul Cassirer; then, however, punctually and with regularity I delivered a volume year by year.

Strictly speaking, I made only one resolve in all my life, that of becoming an art historian. All other decisions have been made by others, by such energetic gentlemen as Bode and Hitler.

Quentin Massys as Genre Painter

IN THE MIDDLE AGES the practice of art was a craft, but a craft which raised itself above other manual occupations insofar as it served spiritual instead of earthly needs. The artist had something in common with the priest, even though by his activity he, more decidedly than the clergy, was directed to the reality provided by the senses, since he could represent the spiritual only through the corporeal, thought only through the visual.

When in the course of the fifteenth century the visual arts loosened their relationship to the Church, and when, in the sixteenth, secular types of pictures began to emerge, tradition and custom still held the painter under the ban, if not of religion, at least of a moral principle which emanated from the Church.

In the beginnings of genre painting there is to be observed an outward as well as an inner bond with religious art. One descended from the celestial and approached earthly life which, seen from above, appeared sinful.

In heaven all is harmonious, static, enduring, calm; on earth all is conflicting, dynamic, restless. As there is only one straight road, but many roundabout ways, so there is only one repose, but many kinds of unrest, only one perfect form, but deformity in divers shapes. The multiplicity of earthly things, their individuality, attracted the artist and served as a contrast which enhanced the effect of the celestial, the changeless, the typical. Genre painting began therewith to chastise the earthly in the form of ugliness.

An Adriaen van Ostade, a Jan Steen, were the first to stand on the same ground as the men whose actions and impulses they let pass, on which they did not express judgment. Not until the

Quentin Massys, The Business Transaction
Staatliche Museen der Stiftung Preussischer Kulturbesitz, Berlin (Dahlem)

seventeenth century did pure genre come to flourish, from a neutral contemplation of daily existence. The card and chess games, the society scenes that Lucas van Leyden painted, are noteworthy forerunners. The oppressive and gloomy mood not in accord with pleasures is more and more eliminated.

The Master of the Female Half-Figures represents women reading, writing, making music, like Gerard Terborch, but he never forgets to add an ointment jar as an excuse, in order to indicate the penitent Magdalene. Here is an outward connection with the religious picture.

In front of the genre pictures of Quentin Massys which are

known, it is usual to speak of satire, of a moralizing tendency, and of caricature. This master was older than Lucas van Leyden and grew up in the orthodox atmosphere of Louvain before he moved, about 1490, to the commercial port of Antwerp. His genre had its origin in the altar picture, in scenes of the Passion and of martyrdom. In the right wing of his Antwerp altarpiece, St. John the Evangelist endures his martyrdom crowded round by creatures maliciously jeering and lusting for blood. Equally dramatic is the contrast between suffering saintliness and active mass-hysteria illustrated in the little-known Ecce Homo panel which was acquired some time ago by the Prado from a Spanish private collection. This Passion panel in Madrid is distinguished by its unusual composition. While Massys by preference spreads his figures relieflike in one plane, here he crowds the thick group of forms diagonally into the depth. The solid series of heads thrusts in a sharp angle toward the side borders. Since the master here, however, as always, is concerned with nothing so much as the intensity of the physiognomies, no true effect of depth results. The logic of space is sacrificed to the wish to set as many actors as possible on the picture surface close to the spectator, providing a chart of specimens of pitiless, malicious, jeering men, their faces distorted by fury.

Massys, who endowed his saints and chosen ones with dignity and beauty, but saw the nameless crowd as swayed by sensual, base impulses, took the attitude of admonisher in his genre pictures, as one who warned against folly and avarice. To be sure, the sermon overflowed into comic entertainment, and as such found acceptance, approval, and success. Extreme deformity became a means for sensational effect.

Massys, unlike Jan Gossaert, was not diverted from his course in Italy; rather he met Leonardo on his way. His taste for refinement, for ladylike femininity, as well as his delight in physiognomical curiosities, was, if not aroused, at least strengthened and enhanced through the southern prototype. It is obviously after "Caricatures" of Leonardo that he executed the bust of the frightfully ugly old woman that came to light in a British private collection, as well as the signed profile head of a brutal man in the Jacquemart-André Collection in Paris, in which the penwork of the Italian was transposed into a detailed, three-dimensional, and material reality. It was reserved for a Netherlander to take so seriously and make use of the pictorial fancies of Leonardo. No Italian would have thought of it.

If we survey the paintings of Quentin that are called genre pictures, because a more suitable term is lacking, it is not always easy to grasp what the master wished to create, and what his contemporaries thought in looking at them. The best-known original, "The Gold-Weigher and his Wife" in the Louvre, least like a caricature among the master's genre pictures, may contain an unobtrusive admonition. While the man blessed with possessions appears absorbed in his occupation, his wife, who is turning the pages of a prayer book, is distracted from her devotions to glance at the worldly activity of the husband. Pious contemplation is interrupted by materialistic impulse.

In other paintings by Quentin, often preserved only in copies, the contrasts are more sharply pointed with dramatic comedy. Particularly popular was the type of picture representing the "Ill-Matched Lovers," which Massys created under the inspiration of Leonardo. At least one picture of this theme is recognized as an original, namely the one in the collection of the Countess Pourtalès in Paris. An old man whose head is stamped with vice, his features distorted by lust, seeks to embrace a girl who smiles engagingly and strokes his fat chin, while she hands the purse of the bemused lover to a fellow who wears a fool's cap. As for the companion-piece, the love-starved old woman who buys the affection of a young man, there is, as far as I know, no authentic painting of the master known. A composition on this theme, with many figures, which was on the Vienna art market in 1930, reveals particularly clearly the connection with Leonardo's "Caricatures" (Cf. the drawing in Windsor, reproduced by Von Seidlitz, *Leonardo da Vinci,* I, p. 256.) It was Cranach who thoroughly exploited this erotic motif, which he had presumably become acquainted with during his stay in the Netherlands.

Money as the source of social evils, as the motive of tragi-comic scenes, also dominates two genre pictures that are considered originals by Quentin—in Rome and in the Berlin Gallery. The one in the Doria Collection shows four men close together, two tax collectors or usurers—one of them fat and satisfied, the other malevolent—and their debtors, whom they are pressing hard. One of the debtors despairingly makes a payment, while the second nods his head and tries to smile. Just as psychologically overcharged is the picture acquired a few years ago for the Museum in Berlin, for which the catalogue gives the title, "The Business Transaction." Three swindlers, representing three temperaments, are persuading a fat burgher to sign a paper. The stout fellow beams as though good luck is befalling him, while the expressions and gestures of the scoundrels leave no doubt that he is being cheated. Stupidity falls victim to crafty calculation. Contrasts abound in this type of picture: the spiritual versus the sensual, beauty of form versus deformity, youth versus age, stupidity versus cunning.

Extraordinarily often there appears, mostly in inferior copies, a composition with two monks, of whom one, with his head in strictly frontal view, has folded his hands and appears to be devoutly praying. The other turns half-sideways to lay his hand on the shoulder of his brother. The meaning of this scene remains obscure to us, but it must have been understandable to the contemporaries of the master. The best example of this composition, one which became known to me in the London art market, can hardly be the original by Quentin's hand. On one copy may be read the inscription: *Bonum est prestolari cum silentio salutare dei.*

I can add two genre pictures of Quentin to those that are

known. In the art market I came across the bust of a repulsive old woman seen frontally, and in Paris recently the half-figure of a bagpiper turned up. An old woman with naked breast is mentioned in the inventory of the art treasurers of the Archduke Leopold Wilhelm. (Cf. Brising, *Quentin Massys,* Upsala, 1909, p. 106.) The musician is painted in oil on paper. A laughing old man, executed in the same technique, is mentioned in 1616 as "extremely well done by Master Quentin." (Brising, in the same passage.) The picture in Paris, perhaps a study, perhaps a fragment of a composition, exudes self-satisfied sensuality. The head, with the powerful double chin, strongly hooked nose which droops to the swollen lower lip, the small, deep-set eyes, is crowded in a narrow picture surface together with the fat hands, one of which is raised in gesticulation.

Without taking the grotesque into consideration, our understanding of Quentin's art remains incomplete. W. Bürger (*Gaz. des B-A,* 1861) has aptly said, *"Les conceptions embrassent le haut et le bas de l'humanité, le côté tragique et le côté burlesque."* Somewhat boldly, he then couples Massys with Rembrandt, the "Dutch Shakespeare." This honor, if granted at all, ought to be reserved for Pieter Brueghel. What the ambitious virtuoso lacked was naiveté, unselfconsciousness, the compulsion of genius.

Berlin Art Collectors

THE PAINTING collectors, almost all stimulated more or less by Bode, were namely, James Simon, E. Simon, M. Kappel, L. Koppel, Oscar Huldschinsky, Carl Hollitscher, R. von Kaufmann. It is worth nothing that all were Jews by race, furthermore, that Kappel and Von Kaufmann were Rhinelanders (as were Von Carstanjen and Von Beckerath also), Koppel was a Saxon, Huldschinsky was from Schleswig, Hollitscher from Austria, thus only the Simon cousins were Berliners. In all these gentlemen who were spurred on by Bode's activity, the incentives, in this or that combination, were social ambition, sublimated love of splendor and enjoyment of art, and also, in the case of R. von Kaufmann, shrewd speculation, justifiable expectation of a rise in value.

The golden age of the private collection in Berlin was short, essentially coinciding with and dependent upon Bode's effectiveness in the museums, beginning about 1880 and ending with the inflation, that is, 1920. Independent of Bode were O. Hainauer, who acquired Italian Renaissance works very early, Von Carstanjen (Dutch paintings of the seventeenth century), and A. von Beckerath (Italian sculpture, drawings). B. Oppenheim, the knowledgeable collector of German sculpture, was free from Bode's influence, as were the collectors of decorative art Eugen Gutmann and Dr. G. Reichenheim. Apart from the Von Carstanjen collection, which went through purchase to the Cologne Museum, and the drawings in Von Beckerath's possession, which were taken over by the Berlin Print Room, everything was dispersed, and the greater part vanished out of Germany.

103

O. Hainauer had learned from the Rothschilds that the only respectable way to show increasing wealth was in the form of precious works of art. The Jews wanted to appear not only rich, but cultivated and on a high intellectual level. The old nobility, thanks to its power, could reveal its wealth in the extent of its landed property. Moreover, the Jews, whose ancestors had been pedlars and money-changers, had a special talent for appreciating visible values and knew how to take care of movable possessions. Bode promoted private collecting so intensively, he recommended, he advised, in the first place because he thereby enhanced his power in the art market, and secondly because he looked for thanks in the form of gifts and bequests to his museums. In the latter he was only partly successful; the World War and inflation crushed many of his hopes. Of the old Berlin collections the only one to be preserved was that of L. Koppel, which the son Albert, still substantially in possession of his father's great fortune, took at the right time to Zurich, and thence to America. For a short period the Berliners, made ambitious and liberal through Bode, were the most important potential participants on the international art market, especially before the rich South Africans, like A. Beit, Wernher, the Neumanns, stepped in as competitors, and before the invincible P. Morgan invaded the scene.

Notes

1 The passage is found in a letter of Schinkel's dated August 6, 1816, from Heidelberg, to the Legation Counselor Eichhorn (from Schinkel's *Nachlass*, II, Berlin, 1862, pp. 182 ff.).

2 Ralph Nicholson Wornum (1812-1877), who in 1863 was the first to dispute the authenticity of the Dresden picture, was from 1853 Keeper and Secretary of the National Gallery. He was a friend of Ruskin, to whom he dedicated his *Some Account of the Life and Works of Hans Holbein,* London, 1867, and is granted to be the founder of English scientific art criticism. Since in his lifetime there was as yet no art scholarship in the present-day sense, he could be designated as a "dilettante" in the sense in which the term was applied to the fathers of German art scholarship. For the controversy on the two Holbein Madonnas see, above all, A. von Zahn, "Die Ergebnisse der Holbein-Ausstellung in Dresden," in *Jahrbücher für Kunstwissenschaft,* ed. Dr. A. von Zahn, V. Leipzig, 1873, pp. 147 ff. and 193 ff.: also Adolph Bayersdorffer, "Der Holbein-Streit," in *A. Bayersdorffer, Leben und Schriften,* Munich, 1902, pp. 133 ff. Cf. the appreciation which Friedländer extends to Bayersdorffer in his *On Art and Connoisseurship,* Boston, Beacon Press, 1960, pp. 13, 14, as well as pp. 232-34 for the Holbein controversy.

3 Perhaps the "P" means Wilhelm Pinder who, in 1940, in the foreword to the third and fourth editions of his *Kunst der deutschen Kaiserzeit,* wrote: "Our history has changed so violently since the appearance of the first edition (1935), that not a few passages of the text are overreached. A thoroughgoing alteration would require time which the author does not at the moment have at his disposal. Only when the final shaping of Europe can be surveyed in quiet, then only can the adjustment be carried out, which will also apply for this book."

4 The "prophetic"passage of Justi is found in his *Winckelmann und seine Zeitgenossen,* 2nd ed., Leipzig, 1898, p. 237, and reads: "After the new French realism had done away with the outmoded conception

of art as one of the vehicles of expression of the human spirit, and soon even action, form, and the entire interesting human refuse came to be regarded as only the inconvenient accessory to an artful capture of colored or colorless vapor, as the goal of painting, one could foresee that shortly thereafter the need for the adoration of more or less unintelligible symbols would arise, preferably in the cloak of the unnatural, or the anti-natural, as the really artistic. After Pallas and the Muses had relinquished their place to Marsyas and his charming crowd, the time now seemed ripe for the ape Haneman and his profound spiritual and ghostly phantoms; and this also will probably, even before these words are printed and read, sink into the 'twilight of the idols.' "

5 *Neue Beiträge Deutscher Forschung,* to Wilhelm Worringer on his sixtieth birthday, edited by Erich Fidder, Königsberg, 1943.

6 Gertrud Staats (Feb. 21, 1859-June 21, 1938) was a landscape painter in Breslau. The Director of the Breslau Gallery, Mueller Hofstede, in the year 1938, arranged a memorial exhibition of her work.

7 Friedländer has incorporated these remarks on Huxley in *Landscape, Portrait, Still-Life, Their Origin and Development,* New York, Schocken Books, 1963, p. 72.

8 The quotation in Thomas Mann, *Betrachtungen eines Unpolitischen,* Berlin, 1919, pp. 477 ff., reads: "Jensen calls to mind the importance of the Jews to the overall development of the Reich—these hardened children of misfortune whose being was thrust together with the German spirit reared through misfortune in another way. But it was this very collision that ground the character of the German people so fine that at present it is the sharpest, most perfect moral apparatus the world has ever seen. 'The soul's struggle to live,' says Jensen, 'has in both parties startled the innermost capacities out of the vegetative twilight, has spurred all noble and ignoble passions, has summoned every reserve, with the collective result of work and more work. An education such as Germany has experienced through the incorporation of Jewish elements into its national body is without any counterpart; on both sides the psychological tension is brought out in such hair-fine, sharp nuances that in the last ten years it has been almost painful to become familiar with German intellectual productions.' "

106

9 Friedländer is probably thinking of the passage in *Der grüne Heinrich,* I, Stuttgart and Berlin, 1910, p. 369: "The performance was based on Schiller's 'Tell,' which was frequently to be found in a school edition in which only the love episode between Berta von Bruneck and Ulrich von Rudenz was missing. The book is very familiar to the people, for it expresses in a wonderful way their sentiment and everything they hold to be thoroughly true; how, then, a mortal will rarely take it amiss if he is idealized a little poetically, or even a great deal."

10 Friedländer probably means the self-description of the poet Axel Martini in Thomas Mann's *Königliche Hoheit,* Berlin, 1910, pp. 233 ff.: "In order to produce such a poem from time to time—who, I wonder, believes how much indolence, ennui, and morose idleness is necessary. A postcard to the cigar-seller is often a day's accomplishment. One sleeps a lot, one lolls about with a dull head. Yes, it is not infrequently a dog's life . . ."

11 The passage is in *Menschliches Allzumenschliches,* Kröner ed., Werke II, 1930, pp. 304 ff., Aphorism 475: "The whole problem of the Jews is to be found only within the national states, insofar as here everywhere their activity and higher intelligence, their accumulated capital of spirit and will, schooled in long suffering from generation to generation, must gain ascendency in a measure arousing envy and hatred, so that in almost all present-day nations literal bad conduct is taking the upper hand—and, to be sure, the more nationalistically they behave —to sacrifice the Jews as scapegoats for every possible public and domestic evil. As soon as it is no longer a question of the conservation of nations, but of generating a compound European race of the utmost strength, then the Jew as an ingredient is just as useful and desirable as any other national remnant. Every nation, every human being, has disagreeable, indeed dangerous, characteristics; it is cruel to demand that the Jew should be an exception. Those characteristics in him may even be dangerous and frightening in a special measure; and perhaps the youthful Jew of the purse-strings is the most offensive invention of the entire human race. Nevertheless, I should like to know how much, in the total reckoning, one must overlook in a people that, not without the fault of all of us, has had the most sorrowful history among all peoples, and to which one owes the noblest human being (Christ), the purest philosopher (Spinoza), the mightiest Book, and

the most effective moral law in the world. Moreover, in the darkest time of the Middle Ages, when the Asiatic cloud had spread itself oppressively across Europe, it was Jewish freethinkers, scholars, and physicians who, under the severest personal constraint, held fast the banner of enlightenment and of intellectual independence and who defended Europe against Asia. It is thanks not least of all to their pains that a more natural, more rational, and in any case unmythical explanation of the world finally could again triumph, and that the ring of the culture that links us now with the enlightenment of Greco-Roman Antiquity remained unbroken. When Christianity has done everything to orientalize the Occident, so has Judaism helped essentially to occidentalize it again and again—which, in a definite sense, is as much as to say, helped to make Europe's mission and history a continuation of that of Greece."

12 Aphorism 109 in *Menschliches Allzumenschliches* II, "Der Wanderer und sein Schatten" (p. 227), 1886: "The Treasure of German Prose —If one looks beyond Goethe's writings and especially Goethe's *Conversations with Eckermann,* the best German book there is, what actually remains of German prose literature, that should deserve to be read again and again? Lichtenberg's *Aphorismen,* the first book of Jung-Stilling's *Lebensgeschichte,* Adalbert Stifter's *Nachsommer,* and Gottfried Keller's *Leute von Seldwyla*—and there, for the time being, is the end."

13 Stefan Zweig died on February 22, 1942, in Petropolis, Brazil, by his own hand.

14 Moritz Busch noted in his *Tagebuchblätter* (Leipzig, 1899), II, under January 10, 1871, p. 33, as a statement of Bismarck's: "By the way, it is probably better the other way round—when one mates a Christian stallion of German stock with a Jewish mare. The currency must come into circulation again, and also it produces no bad race. I do not know what I shall advise my sons." Since Busch was an anti-Semite, and Bismarck read the correction proofs of Busch's work before it came out, the authenticity of the statement is not to be doubted.

15 The views of Nietzsche on the Jews are compiled in R. M. Lonsbach, *Nietzsche und die Juden,* Stockholm, 1939.

16 The passage in Justi reads: "Although already dominated early by the idea of a 'system,' he (Winckelmann) nevertheless proceeds according to so broad a method of aphorisms, as if there were no great hurry with that system. This is certainly to the advantage of the work, for once the system exists, then the windows of observation tend to close."

17 Hermann Beenken, *Hubert und Jan van Eyck,* Munich, 1941.

18 Thomas Mann, *Betrachtungen eines Unpolitischen,* Berlin, 1919, p. 192: "An art movement (Expressionism) of violently active demands, contemptuously averse to repose, to contemplation, to epic ease, to objectivity and serenity, completely bent on the rapid, the vehemently agitated, the shockingly expressive—requires one day that 'the intellectual man act.' That could be a good thing. As for me, I remember with interest and gratitude precious, in the Goethe sense, 'significant' impressions of the bursting fury, the ferocity, wild garishness, harshness, inquietude, the mercilessness, viciousness and inhumanity with which certain contemporary stories are told, and I say to myself: 'Whether the political dogma of these colleagues is pacifistic or not matters little—the war is here!' They sang it in every line, before it was here, and never was there a better example of how little the thinking proclaims the being. And does not their own confession, their own pride, correspond to my clear insight? An Expressionist leader, of the painters, however, not the literary men, proclaimed in August, 1914: 'This is our hour!' "